HOW TO DEVELOP MENTAL SKILLS FOR COMPETITIVE EXAMS

(JEE, NEET, CUET, UPSC, ICAR, JET, NDA, NTSE, KVPY ETC.)

ACHARYA VISHVENDRA

Dedicated to the problems i faced during my JEE preparation,and the efforts to resolve them with success in getting admission in government college of technology,pantnagar,uttrakhand without any formal coaching on the basis of self study.

Contents

Foreword

Preparationof competitive exams like **JEE,NEET,UPSC,CUET,ICAR,NTSE,KVPY** is a challenging task.Challenge is not about the complexities of subjects.But its about the emotional conflicts one face.

Any competitive exam checks your "**MIND-BRAIN SYSTEM**" through multiple dimensions involving **memory,decision making,analysis,problem solving skills,will power** etc.But in formal education systems,the focus is only on **memory**.there are just a **few patterns** which are repeated again and again.As an impact most of the students have the experience of working with **memory only**.and this exposure is **sufficient** as per formal school education is concerned but to deal with competitive exams,this is the first step,students must have exposure to other functions of the "**MIND-BRAIN SYSTEM**" too which involves Problem solving skills,decision making,visualization,strong will power,calculation skills,optimal performance skills.

All these skills play the central role for a student in being successful in cracking a competitive exam but there is no focus on developing these mental skills.as an impact most of the students preparing for competitive exams fail in them.

This book is written to make students learn the **mental skills** required to crack competitive exams like **JEE,NEET,UPSC,CUET,ICAR,NTSE,KVPY** so that they **ACTUALLY** prepare for competitive exams rather than just **ACTING** to prepare.

Preface

Most of the students preparing for **competitive exams** fail in them?only a **few special students** are able to qualify them.What is so **special** about the **successful students?**do they have some **secret book** to prepare?do they know something which others **don't know?**do they have access to some **highly classified information** or they just have a better "**MIND-BRAIN SYSTEM**" having some **different mental skills** which most of the students **don't have.**

This book is an attempt to focus on **developing the mental skills** which are the foundation step for cracking any competitive exam like **JEE,NEET,UPSC,CUET,ICAR,NTSE,KVPY.**

Acknowledgements

Thanks to the quest to know beyond **INFORMATION** and thinking in terms of **SKILLS.**

Prologue

cracking a competitive exam like **JEE,NEET,UPSC,CUET,ICAR,NTSE,KVPY** is not as easy as it seems to be.Those students who qualify these exams have some **special mental skills** which other students don't have,success in **competitive exams** is due to these **mental skills** and not because of some hidden **book,formula or concept.**

All students have access to the **information source** these days. Every student preparing himself or in some education systems has access to the same **information source?**but only those students are **successful** who have **mental skills** to process that **huge information** comprising of **several thousand pages.**

This book is explicitly written to train students for learning the **mental skills** for **competitive exams like** JEE,NEET,UPSC,CUET,ICAR,NTSE,KVPY ,so that they **actually prepare** rather than **acting to prepare.**

INTRODUCTION

The most optimised option to earn enough for living a quality life in our country is to qualify a **competitive exam** and get access to **higher education systems.**

FIG-1:QUALITY LIFE

FIG-2: STUDENTS OPT FOR COMPETITIVE EXAMS FOR LIVING A QUALITY LIFE

FIG-3: COMPETITIVE EXAMS IN INDIA

Every year millions of students prepare for competitive exams and compete for a few thousand seats available in these higher education systems.But the slection ratio is very less.For example in **JEE ADVANCED** about only **1.7 percent** of the students qualify for getting a seat in **IITS**.Similarly for **NEET**,the selection ratio is about **2 percent.**

FIG-4: MILLIONS OF STUDENTS PREPARING FOR COMPETITIVE EXAMS

Now the question **arises?**Do the students who qualify these exams have **different brain** than rest of others,or they have some hidden secret books or do they know something which others don't know?

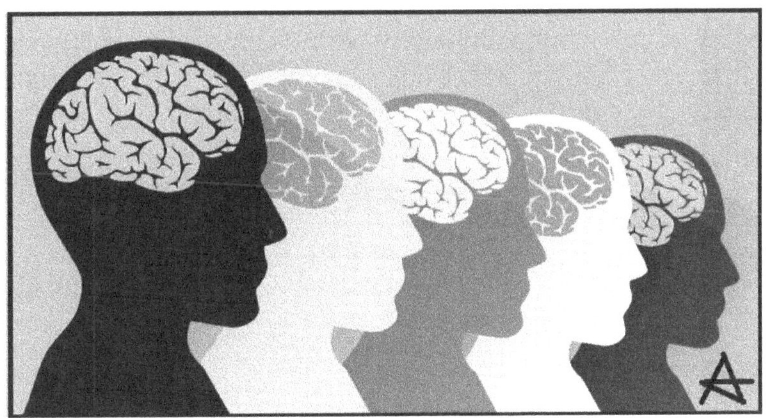

FIG-5: DO THE SUCCESSFUL STUDENTS HAVE SOME DIFFERENT BRAIN?

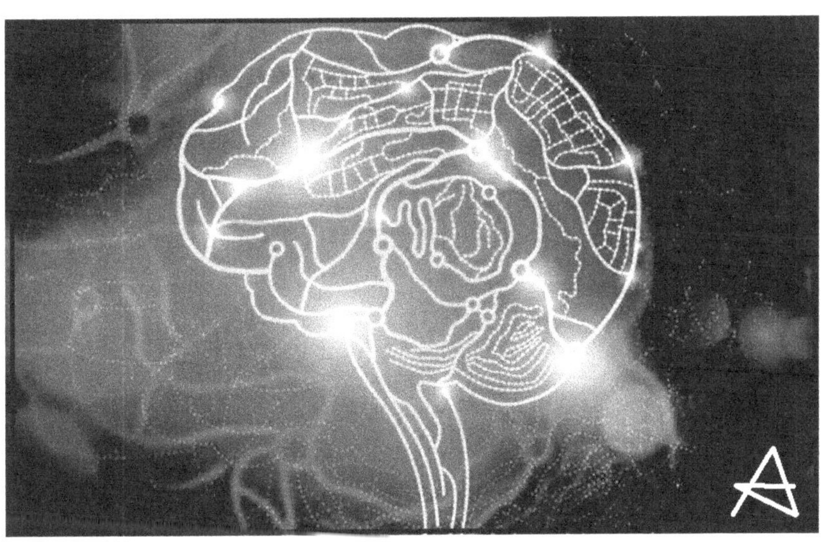

FIG-6: SUCCESSFUL STUDENTS HAVE A BETTER "MIND-BRAIN SYSTEM"

All of us can have different opinions about these questions but we can arrive at a **mutual concensus** that certainly these successful students have a better "**MIND-BRAIN SYSTEM**" than others.

But is that better "**MIND-BRAIN SYSTEM**" god gifted or it can be developed with **systematic preparation**.well we cant do anything about god gifted thing,but certainly i can say that anybody can develop his"**MIND-BRAIN SYSTEM**" working **systematically,analysing and updating strtaegies**,For more details you can refer to the book "developing mind,develop india" .This book is available on amazon.in,flipcart & notionpress.

FIG-7: THE BOOK "DEVELOING MIND,DEVELOP INDIA"

The basis of my saying is my experience as a **jee qualifier,**getting state rank **219 in uttrakhand in JEE MAIN 2007 without any coaching,**getting admission in **government engineering college pantnagar,uttrakhand,**working as a physics faculty for jee & neet in reputed coaching institutes of kota & delhi,working as an author and compiling more than 100 books on **physics,chemistry,mathematics,metaphysics,spiritualism & education pshycology.**

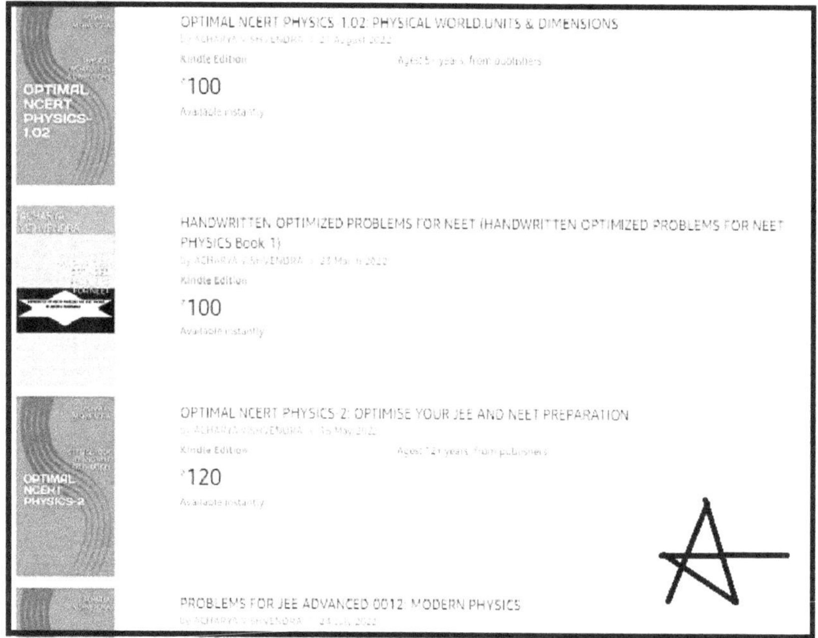

FIG-8: MY BOOKS ON AMAZON.IN

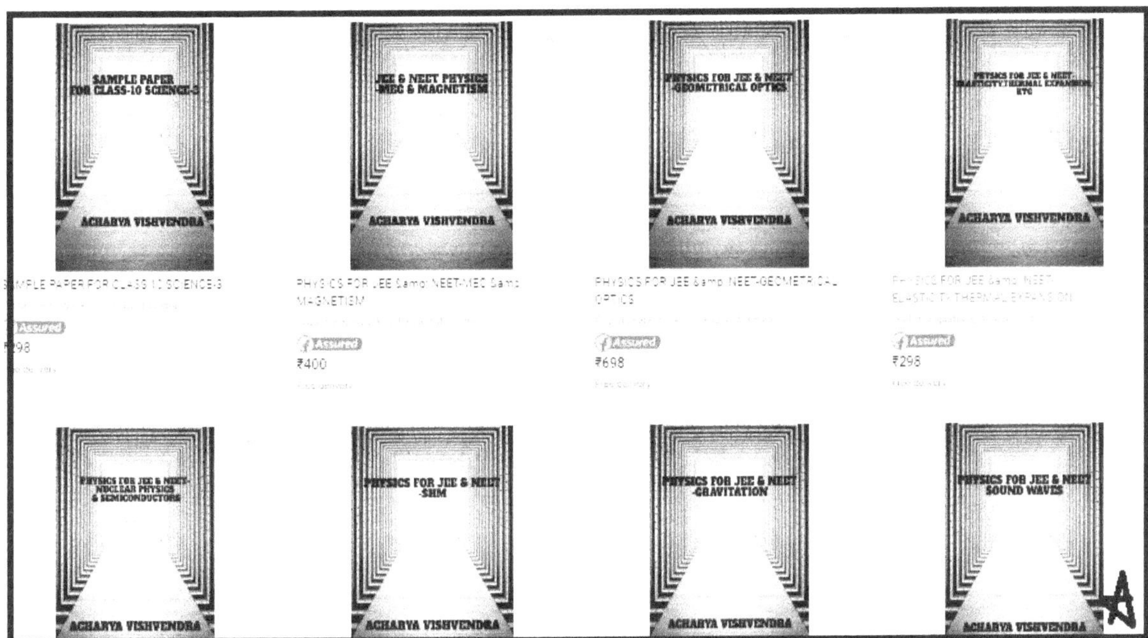

FIG-9: MY BOOKS ON FLIPCART

The process of developing the **"MIND-BRAIN SYSTEM"** is not difficult but different.You have to **overcome** your **traditional belief systems.** our **analytical brain** initially tries to **oppose new learnings.**so you must have a **strong will power** to dominate the analytical brain and be open minded to learn new things as per the requirements.

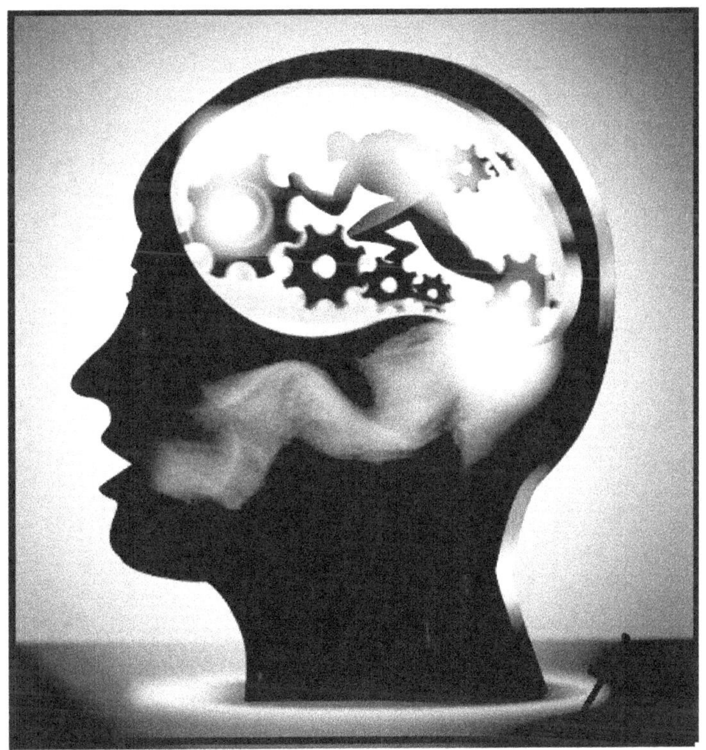

FIG-10: HAVE A STRONG WILL POWER TO DOMINATE ANALYTICAL BRAIN

FIG-11: BE OPEN MINDED TO LEARN NEW THINGS

The various **mental skills** required to crack a **competitive exam** can be listed as:

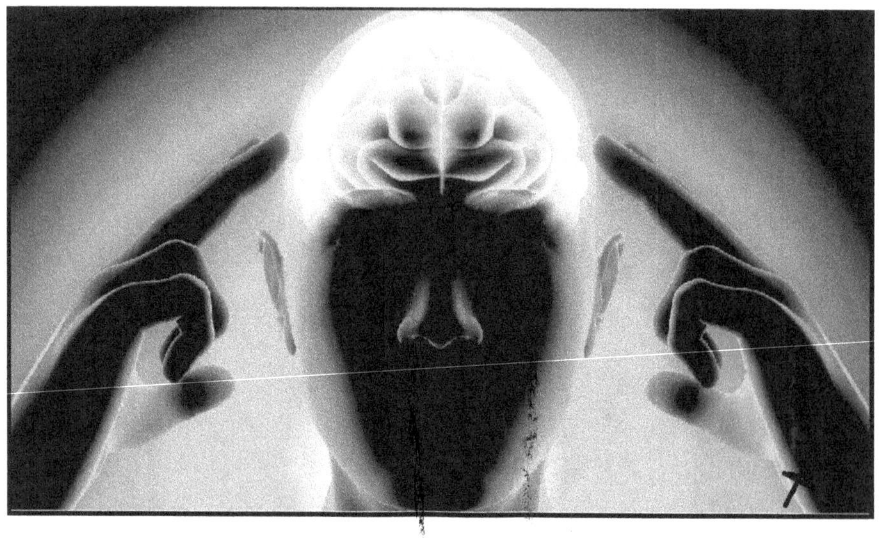

FIG-12: MENTAL SKILLS TO CRACK A COMEPTITIVE EXAM

1.Silent mind skills
2.Information processing skills
3.Analytical skills

4.Visualization skills

5.problem solving skills

6.Optimal performance skills

7.Brainwave frequency modulation skills

8.Strong will power skills

let's discuss each of these skills in the next chapters.

CHAPTER TWO

SILENT MIND SKILL

2.1:Generally a student has a noisy and confused **"MIND-BRAIN SYSTEM".**he is trapped in **information and emotions** of either past or future and is unable to focus on present.

FIG-13: NOISY & CONFUSED MIND OF A STUDENT

So the first **skill** that a student should have is a **silent mind skills.**Silence gives us **power to focus** on **present** rather than being distracted in **past and future.**this power gives us a **stable interior feelings** and we can **learn** and **actually prepare for competitive exam.**

FIG-14: SILENT MIND IS THE FIRST STEP TOWARDS CRACKING A COMPETITIVE EXAM

Generally students have **unstable and noisy mind.**they are **unable to focus** and do the **right work** rather than being **trapped in past or future.**

FIG-15: VARIABLE EMOTIONS OF A STUDENT

FIG-16: CONFUSED MIND OF A STUDENT

2.2:HOW TO LEARN SILENT MIND SKILL:

Any skill takes time to be accepted by our **unconscious mind**.Generally it takes a **minimum of 21 days** to learn a skill.So start with a gradual process of learning and try to learn the new skill in **21 days** time span.

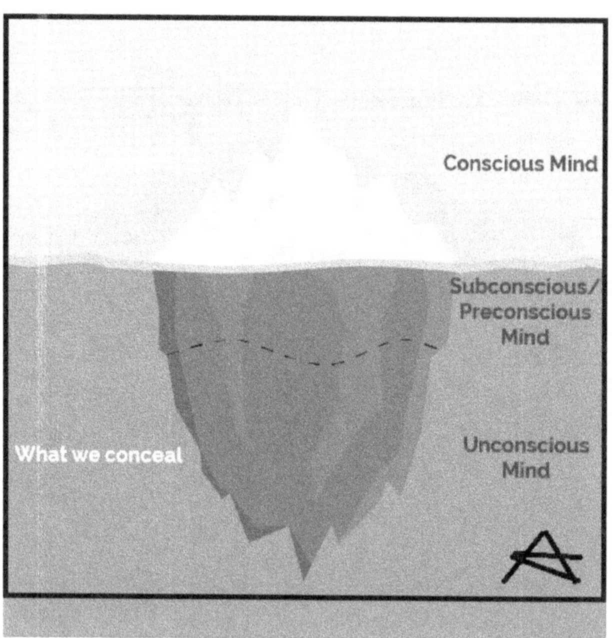

FIG-17: CONSCIOUS,SUB-CONSCIOUS & UNCONSCIOUS MIND

Silence comes with **focus**,focus comes with **increased brainwave frequency**.so **increase your brainwave frequency.**

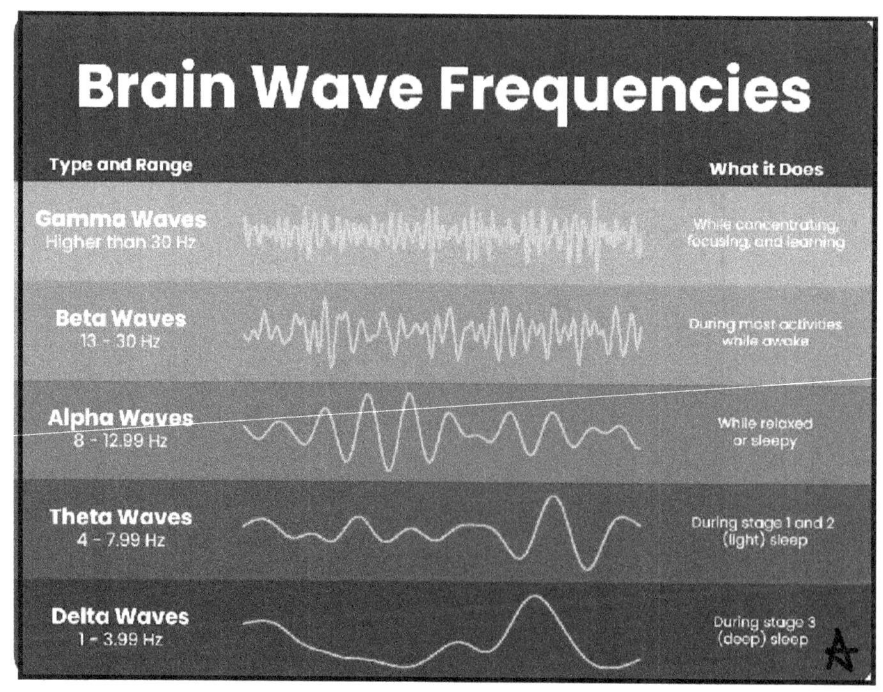

FIG-18: INCREASE YOUR BRAINWAVE FREQUENCY FOR FOCUS & HAVING A SILENT MIND

FIG-19: FOCUS ON PRESENT FOR A SILENT MIND

After increasing your brainwave frequency,you will be naturally focused on present.Start with **5 seconds** initially,during those **5 seconds** try to be **thoughtless and silent**,then **increase this time to 10 seconds,20 seconds,1 inute,5 minute** and at last to somewhat more than **your duration of competitive exams.**For example for **jee & neet** the exam duration is **3 hours** so you should practice with **at least 3.5 hours** so that your **biological clocks and inner mechanisms** are set for **exam duration.**

FIG-20: HAVE A SILENT MIND FOR PROLONGED DURATION

FIG-21: PRACTICE SILENT MIND STATE FOR A DURATION MORE THAN COMPETITIVE EXAM

Its being observed that **most of the students** are not able to **adapt to the long exam duration** and are **unable to achieve optimal results.**make a 21 days diary,daily increase your time and have a target of achieving silent state of mind in 21 days.

S.N.	DATE	SILENT MIND TIME	ANY COMMENT
1.			
2.			
3.			
4.			
5.			
6.			
7.			
8.			
9.			
10.			
11.			
12.			
13.			
14.			
15.			
16..			
17.			
18.			
19.			
20.			
21.			

FIG-22: 21 DAYS PRACTICE FOR LEARNING SILENT MIND SKILL

initially there will be **resistance from your LEFT/ANALYTICAL BRAIN** and you will have to **fight** with the **Analytical brain** to achieve your target.

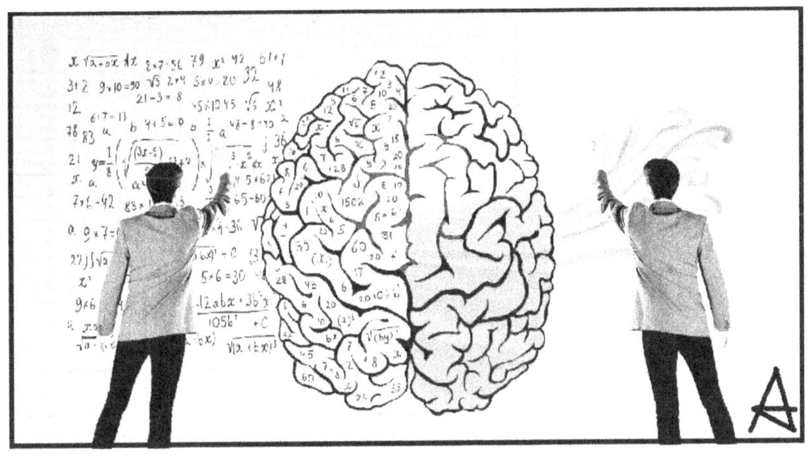

FIG-23: LEFT VERSUS RIGHT BRAIN

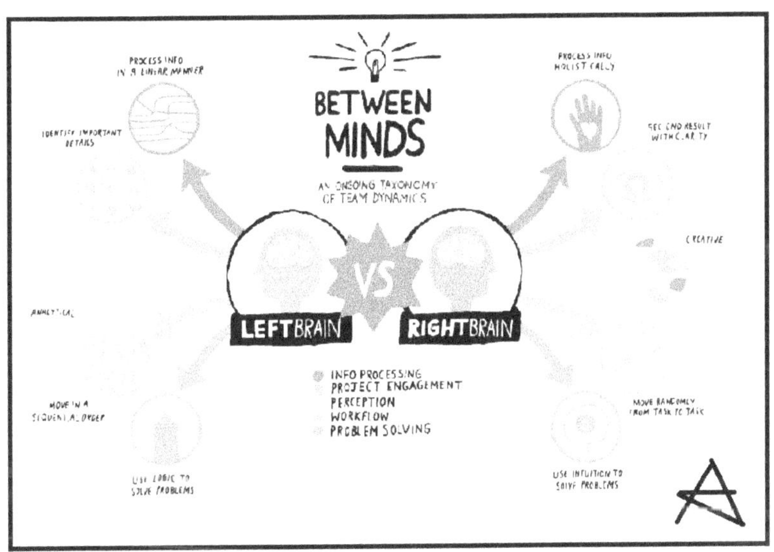

FIG-24: LEFT VERSUS RIGHT BRAIN

we shall deal with the **STRONG WILL POWER SKILLS** in details in the next chapters.

FIG-25: USE STRONG WILL POWER TO DOMINATE ANALYTICAL BRAIN

CHAPTER THREE

INFORMATION PROCESSING SKILL

3.1:INFORMATION PROCESSING SKILLS:

Lets discuss about the **information processing skills now**.These skills are the foundation of your success in competiitve exams like **JEE,NEET,UPSC,CUET,ICAR,NTSE,KVPY**.For being successful you must have **advanced information processing skills.**

3.2:WHY INFORMATION PROCESSING SKILLS ARE MNECESSARY?

Most of the students **fail** in competitive exams because they **dont work** on their **information processing skills**,they just work on **making notes,attending classes,**and just acting to prepare,**mentally** they are in **another dimension** which has nothing to do with the **competitive exams.**The real preparation of competitive exam starts when you start working on your **information processing skills.**

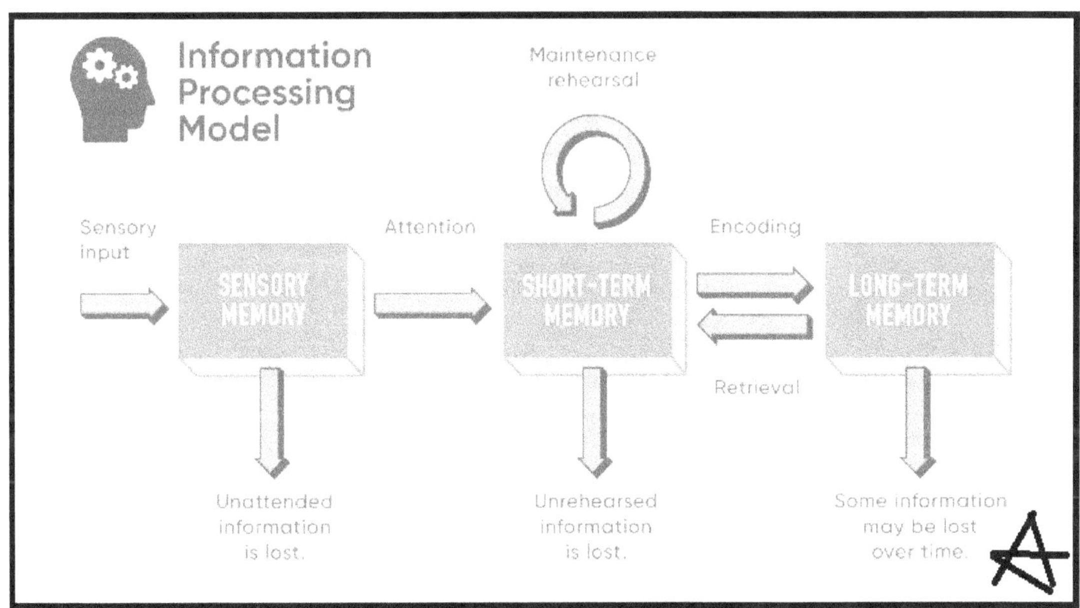

FIG-26: INFORMATION PROCESSING MODEL

3.3:STEPS OF INFORMATION PROCESSING: There are certain steps in information processing skills-

FIG-27: STEPS OF INFORMATION PROCESSING SKILLS

According to the information processing theory, there are four main stages of information processing which include **FOCUSING, ENCODING, STORING, and RETRIEVING.** These four stages are used to describe how the **brain gathers information, processes this information, creates memories, and uses this information when it is needed.**

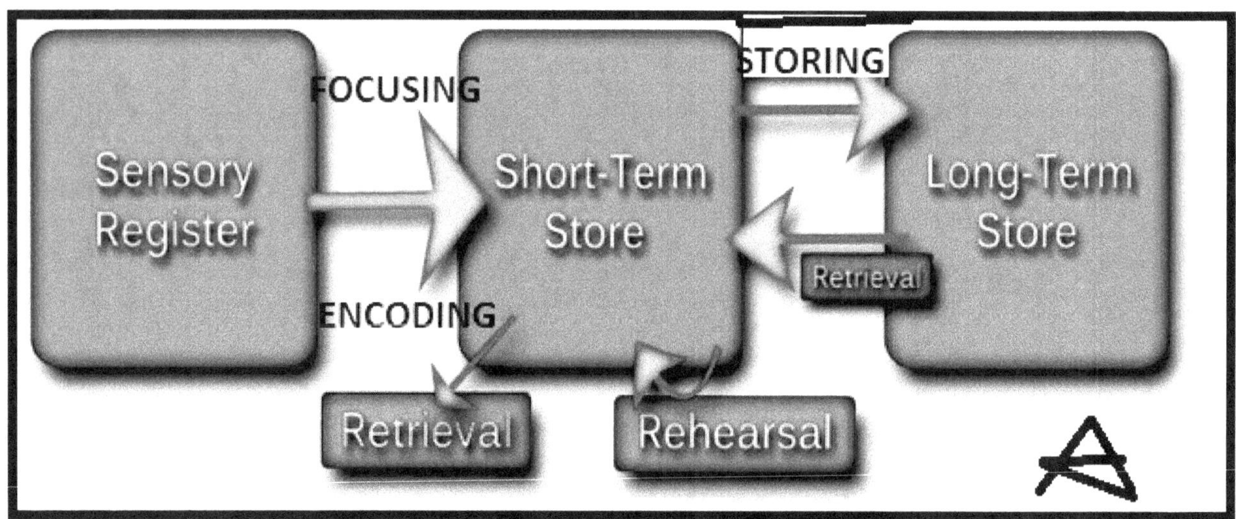

FIG-28: STEPS IN INFORMATION PROCESSING SKILLS

3.3.1:FOCUSING:

Focusing is the **first stage of information processing,** and deals with when a person is gathering information from **external world** and focusing on it.As generally a student is busy in processing some other information in **past or future** so the first step is to focus on the **present** rather than being disturbed in **past or future.** For example, when a student is in classroom ,He is in the **focusing stage** of **information processing.**we are gathering information using our **5 senses,focusing is** the art of being at presemt rather than being disturbed in **past or future.**

FIG-29: FOCUSING

3.3.2:ENCODING/MIND MAPPING:

After focusing we try to **encode/mind map new information** with the **information already present** in our **unconscious mind.**This is done by using an **encoded signal** from **conscious mind to subconscious mind to unconscious mind.**

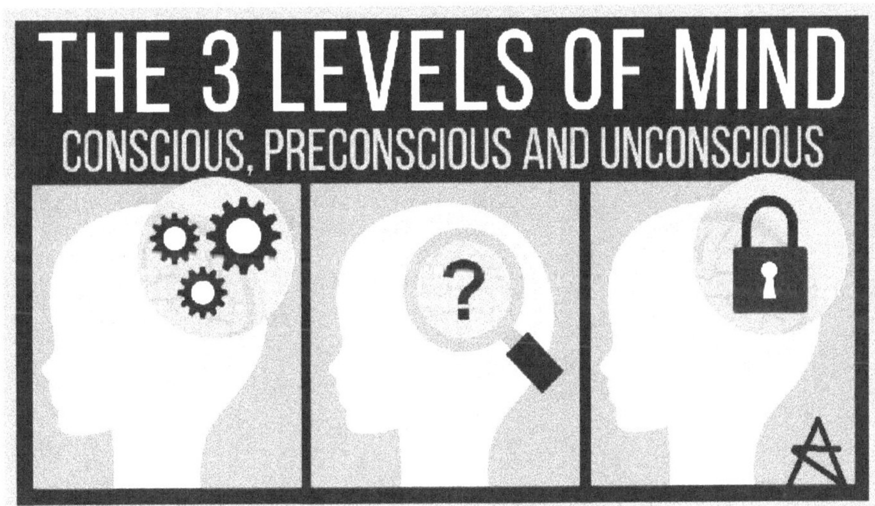

FIG-30: 3 MINDS

This **mind mapping/encoding phenomenon** of **interconnecting the 3 minds** is very important step of **information processing skill** and has to be performed **accurately.**

Have **patience** and wait for the **instant of time** when the **3 minds gets united** and you have a **thoughtless experience.**Hold yourself in this state for at least 10 seconds.

Mind mapping/Encoding is more involved than **focusing.** For example, a student can simply listen to their teacher but if he is unable to **mind map/encode** it with the **unconscius mind** then he will not learn the new information.Hence **encoding/mind mapping** is very crucial.

FIG-31: INTERCONNECTING THE MINDS

Most of the students are not able to process this step.They find it **difficult** to **mind-map/encode new information** with the information in **unconscious mind** and hence are unable to get the **desired result**.hence for getting desierd result students must be an expert in **mind mapping/encoding.**

FIG-32: MIND MAPPING/ENCODING

Once students have laernt the art of **interconnecting the 3 minds** then they canmove on to the next step of processing which is about storing information.

Teaching is effective only when the students have learnt the art of interconnecting the 3 minds.So before getting taught make sure that you have interconnected minds,otherwise you will not be able to learn anything and will just blame others for it where as the problem is within you.

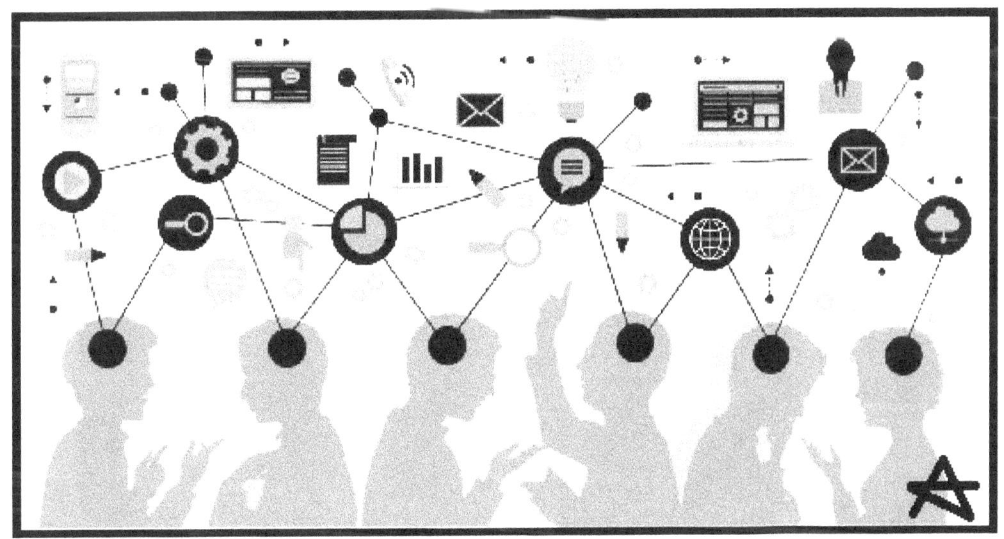

FIG-33: MENTAL INTERACTION BETWEEN A TEACHER AND A STUDENT

most of the students are **unable to interconnect their 3 minds** and hence they are unable to learn effectively and instead of working on the process of interconnecting the minds they find an excuse and blame others for that.Hence students must be an expert in interconnecting the minds and maintain themselves in that mental state for a prolonged time.

3.3.3:STORING:

After **mind mapping/encoding** the nest task is to **store information.**This is an important process and should be handled with care.be thoughtless while storing information and work with **unbroken focus.**

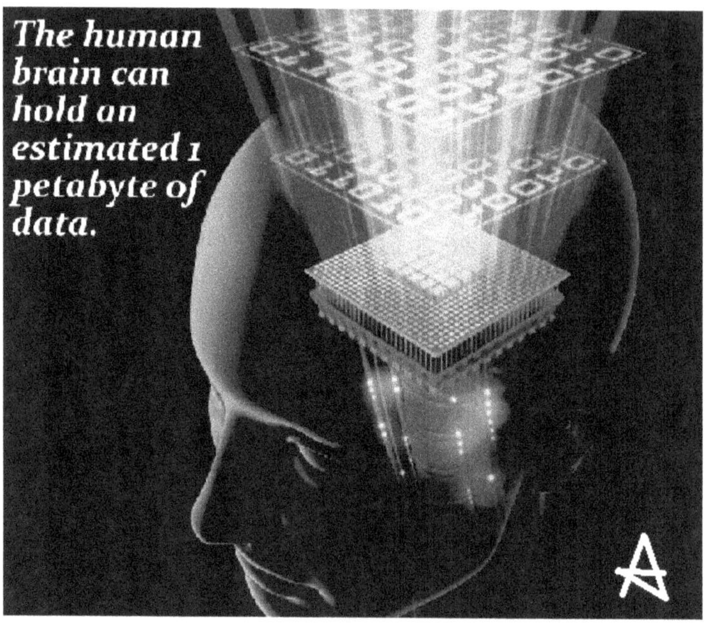

FIG-34: INFORMATION STORAGE IN HUMAN BRAIN

Storing is the third stage of **information processing,** and it deals with the process of storing information in the **"MIND-BRAIN SYSTEM"** for an **extended period of time** at least during **one or 2 years.**

3.3.4:RETRIEVING:

The last but not the least step in information processing is the Retrieving .and it deals with the process when a student remembers information they had stored in their memories some years ago. For example, when a student is giving a **competitive exam,**he is **retrieving information from his brain** along with some **other processes like thinking,naalysis & calculations.**

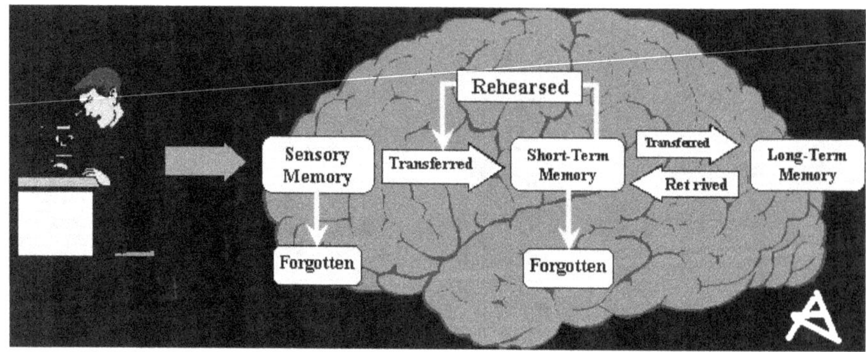

FIG-35: INFORMATION RETRIEVAL FROM HUMAN BRAIN

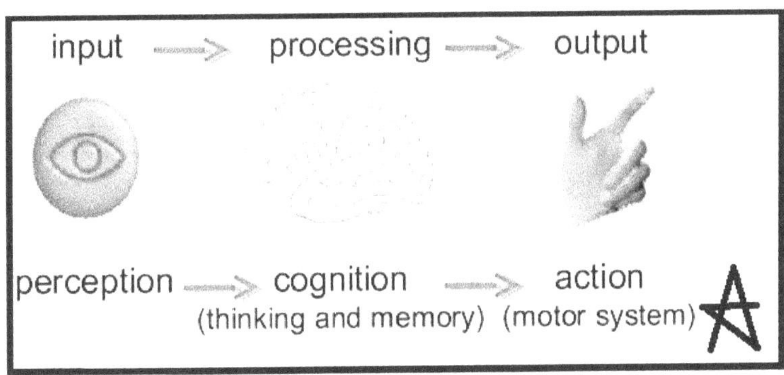

FIG-36: INPUT-PROCESSING AND OUTPUT FOR A HUMAN BRAIN

3.4:DEVELOPING THE PATTERNS:

After **processing information**,Students develops some kind of **patterns** to **retain a set of informations** through which we learn something.These patterns are the actual product of learning.

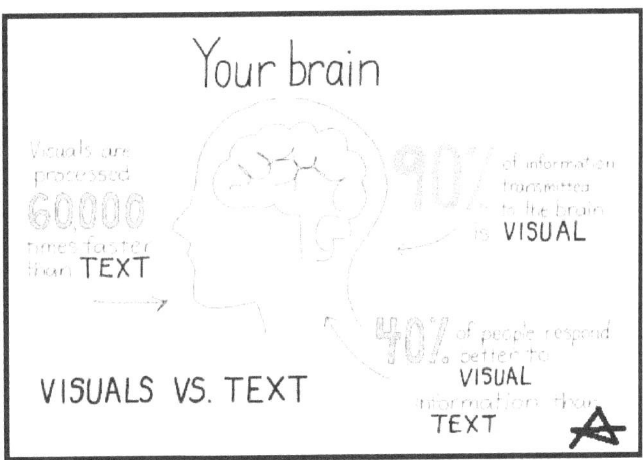

FIG-37: VISUAL & TEXTUAL INFORMATION PROCESSING BY THE BRAIN

Any **competitive exam** is cracked on the basis of these **patterns**.Those students who are successful in **converting the raw information they read through books into a hybrid pattern** are able to **retain as and when needed.**

As an impact of this they are able to solve questions in competitive examwhere as those studenst who are unable to develo the patterns are not able to retain the complete set of infoprmation and hence fails in competitive exams.

hence the entire turning ppoint in the prepartion of competiitve exams is **developing the patterns.**

FIG-38: PATTERNS

FIG-39: PATTERNS DEVELOPED BY SUCCESSFUL STUDENTS

3.5:HOW TO DEVELOP INFORMATION PROCESSING SKILLS?

Information processing skills can't be developed instantly.it takes time to develop these skills.Start with a target of 21 days.

whatever you study,follow a pattern,the pattern is focusing then Mind mapping then information storing and then information retrieving and then repeating the entire process if you are unable to retrieve the information.

Most of the students study without following the pattern,as an impact of which they are unable to retrieve the information when they appear for the examination.Hence **"retrieval" is the main process,hence preparation should be "RETRIEVAL"-ORIENTED.**

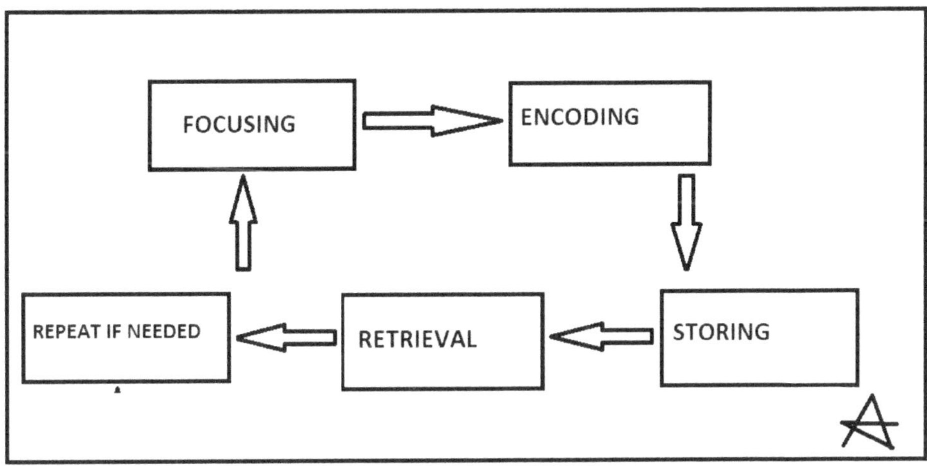

FIG-40: PATTERNS USED BY SUCCESSFUL STUDENTS

Students must clearly understand that how many books you study,how many hours you study?are not significant.The significant thing is your **retrieval capacity.**

Start with a small set of information lets say **1 page of your notes,**but work on that folowing the **algorithm/ pattern.**the pattern is **focusing** then **Mind mapping** then **information storing** and then **information retrieving** and then **repeating the entire process** if you are unable to retrieve the information.After completing the algorithm check your retrieval,repeat the patterns again and again till you are able to retrieve most of the information.

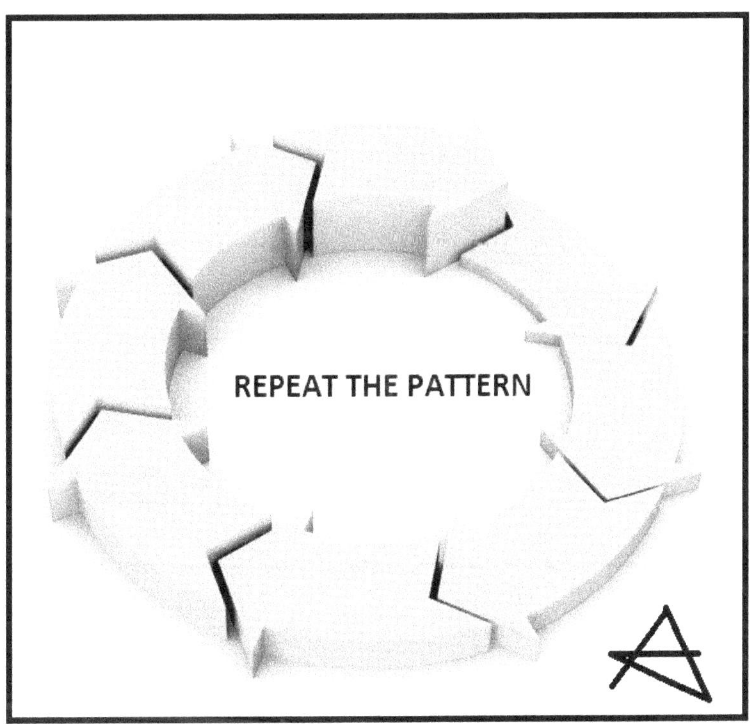

FIG-41: REPEAT THE PATTERNS TILL RETRIEVAL

Practice working on this pattern for 21 days and note down the progress on a sheet as shown below.

S.N.	DATE	FOCUSING	MIND MAPPING/ENCODING	INFORMATION STORING	INFORMATION RETRIEVAL	COMMENTS
1.						
2.						
3.						
4.						
5.						
6.						
7.						
8.						
9.						
10.						
11.						
12.						
13.						
14.						
15.						
16..						
17.						
18.						
19.						
20.						
21.						

FIG-42: REPEAT THE PATTERN FOR 21 DAYS AND NOTE DOWN THE PROGRESS

Your analytical brain will try to disturb you while working on the new pattern.so use will power of needed,but don't leave the pattern in between.if you feel too high resistance from analytical brain.be slow & steady,

if you feel too much resistance and low feelings then meditate to get rid of the negative feelings.For learning meditation you can refer to the book "developing mind-develop india".its available on amazon.in,flipcart & notinpress.

FIG-43: THE BOOK "DEVELOPING MIND-DEVELOP INDIA"

Lets discuss in the next chapter about the next skill which is **analytical skill**

CHAPTER FOUR

ANLYTICAL SKILL

4.1:WHY ANALYTICAL SKILLS ARE REQUIRED?

After developing patterns the next skill which is needed is the **analytical skill.**

To solve problems of **competitive exams** only patterns are **not enough,**you need to **analyse the problem** and recognise the **correct pattern** with which it can be **solved.**This requires **multiple processing** and multiple **parts of the brain.**

Hence analysis is important to solve problems asked in **competitivee exams.**

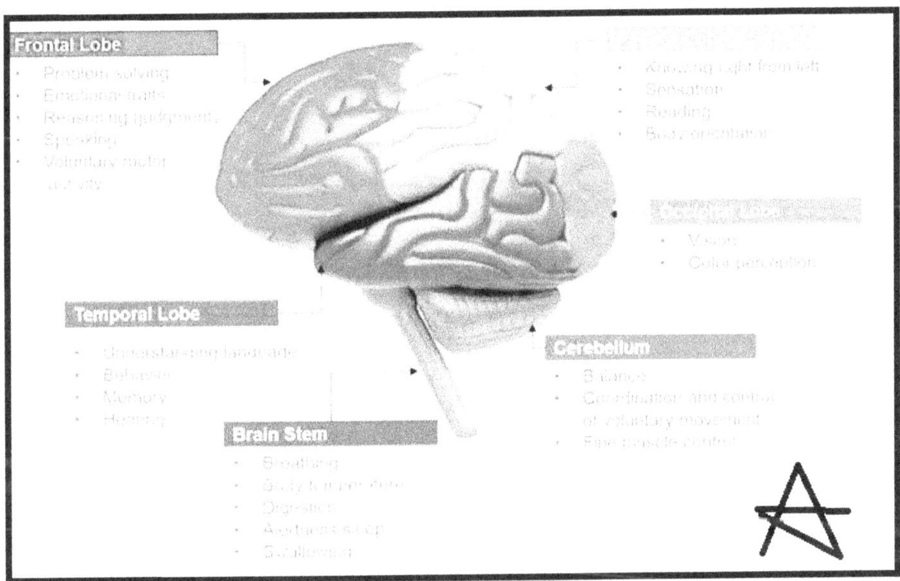

FIG-44:VARIOUS PARTS OF THE BRAIN

FIG-45: A STUDENT ANALYZING PROBLEM & FINDING SOLUTIONS

4.2: HOW TO DEVELOP ANALYTICAL SKILLS?

Analysis is concerned with the **frontal lobe** whereas **memory** is concerned with the **temporal lobe**.so **analysis** is to be integrated with memory and hence its a **multi dimensional task** as you have to switch between using **memory and then analysis**.its necessary to have **proper time gap** between various functions so that each **process** is carried out effectively.

Analytical skills can be developed gradually with proper training.Start with a 21 days target and observe yourself and improve gradually.

S.N.	DATE	SILENT MIND	MIND MAPPING	PATTERN FINDING	CALCULATIONS	COMMENTS
1.						
2.						
3.						
4.						
5.						
6.						
7.						
8.						
9.						
10.						
11.						
12.						
13.						
14.						
15.						
16..						
17.						
18.						
19.						
20.						
21.						

FIG-46: 21 DAYS WORKING TO LEARN ANALYTICAL SKILLS

4.3: APPLICATIONS OF ANALYTICAL SKILLS?

Analytical skills forms an important step in preparing for **competitive exams** as it enables us with the art of choosing the right option out of many options available.Often a problem asked in a **competitive exam** is **multi-dimensional**.There may be **many results concerned with a particular concept**.but which information is to be used?we can decide only by analysing the problem.

For example:In JEE & NEET physics we have equations of motion but we have a total of 3 equations each of which has 5 forms so a total of 3*5=15 options are available.out of which only 1 form is to be used in the exam.

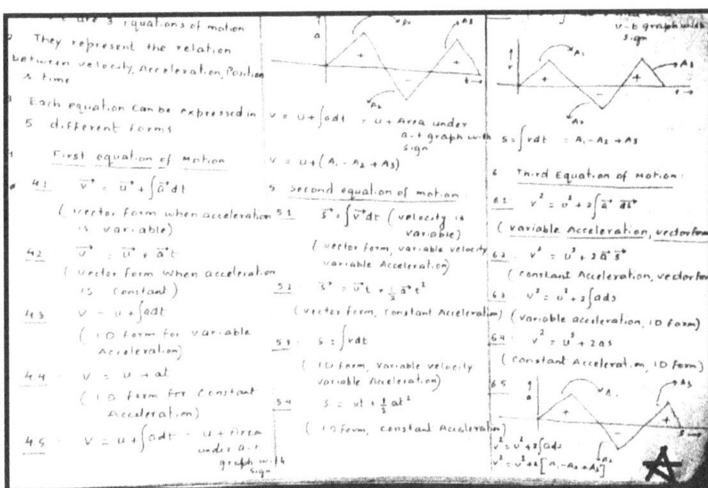

FIG-47: 3 DIFFERENT EQUATIONS OF MOTION IN DIFFERENT FORMS

Analysis gives us the power to decide the right information which is to be used in a particular problem.

FIG-47: STUDENTS TRYING TO FIND SOLUTIONS OF A QUESTION

FIG-48: A STUDENT TRYING TO ANALYSE SOME TOPIC

FIG-49: A STUDENT TRYING TO SOLVE A NEW PROBLEM

Hence we can conclude that analytical skills form an important step in preparing for competitive exams by enabling us with the power to choose the correct information out of a lot of information available.

Lets discuss the next important skill which is the **visualization skill** in the **next chapter**

CHAPTER FIVE

IMAGINATION SKILL

5.1: After developing **analytical skills** the next skill that needs to be learnt for cracking **competitive exams** are imagination skills.

Imagination gives us a direct access to **unconscious mind** while by passing the **analytical brain**,its the gateway to out of box thinking,password to higher dimensions of consciusness.

Sir albert einstein has quoted about imagination as follows:

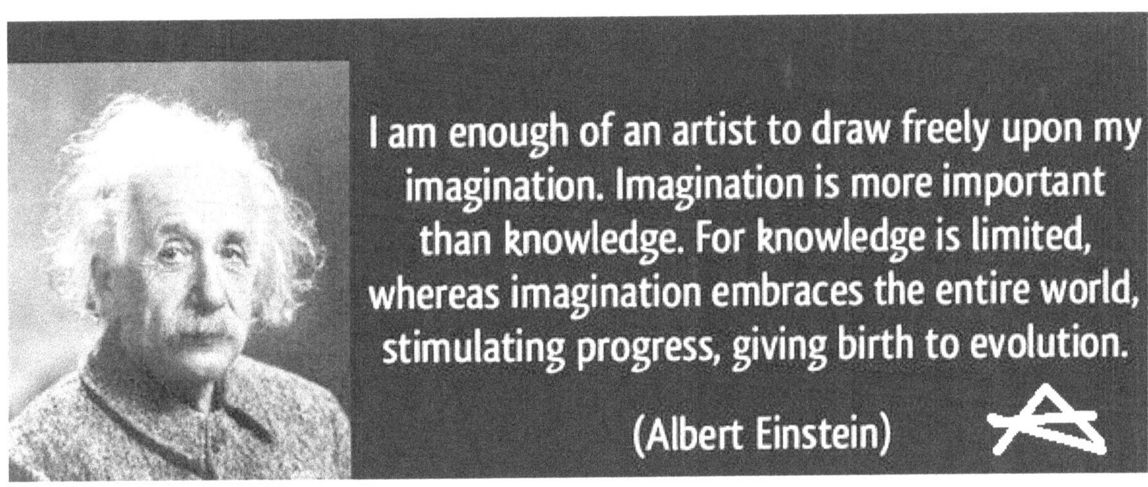

FIG-51: QUOTES OF ALBERT EINSTEIN ABOUT IMAGINATION

In fact the **fundamental source** of every known information is the ability to imagine.**imagination provides** the basis to **develop information** which can be applied to create a better life.

Imagination is to be used in preparing for **competitive exams** but its very necessary to **limit the power of imagination** as you can arrive at a **new result** using imagination,which is not yet published in the **standard books.**As the **solutions** of the questions in **competitive exams** are based on **established facts published** in the **standard books** so its necessary to **cross verify the results** we obtain by **free imagination** and the **standard results** published in **standard books.**

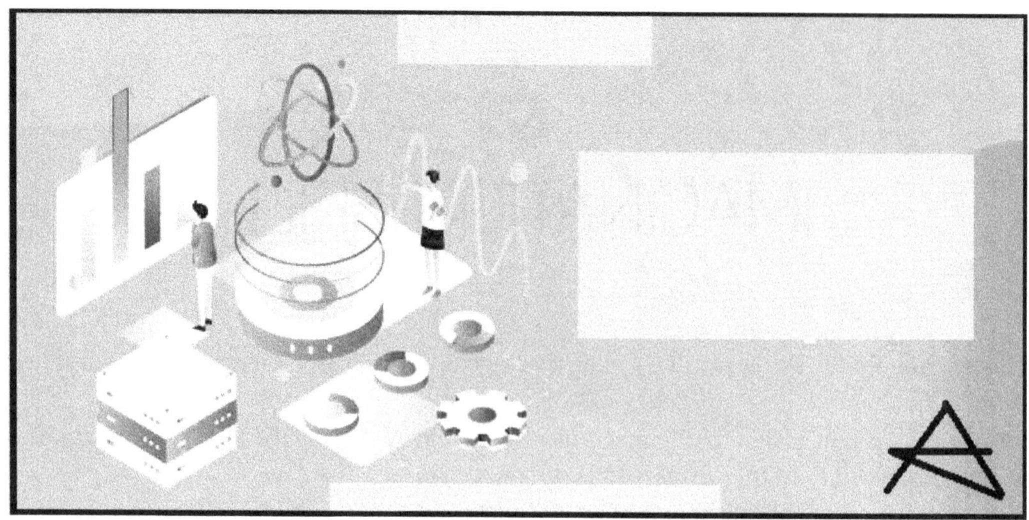

FIG-52: THE RESULTS OF IMAGINATIONS MUST BE MAPPED WITH STANDARD BOOKS

In case of **conflicts between imagination and standard books,**as per **exams** are concerned,we should **stick to the standard fact** which is **globally accepted and published in standard books.**Otherwise you may loose **marks** in the exam.

However if you think that you have decoded some **fundamental law of nature,** then you should work on it **systematically,**develop your **research paper,**collect the **experimental facts** and prepare for **presenatationbefore the concerned authorities.**If you are able to establish your **findings** you will get an "**OUT OF BOX**" reward.

FIG-53: RESERACH PAPER PRESENTATION

It has happened many a times in history when established facts were challenged by new findings,it took time but theories were changed accordingly so as to explain the new observations.For instance,**nature of light** has been **debatable in history,**

initially **sir issac newton** proposed **Particle theory of light** in which he **proposed that light is** made up of particles called **corpuscles** on the basis of **his imaginations cross verified by experiments** on reflection and refraction of light.Because of the **authenticity of his work** light was declared to have **particle nature.**

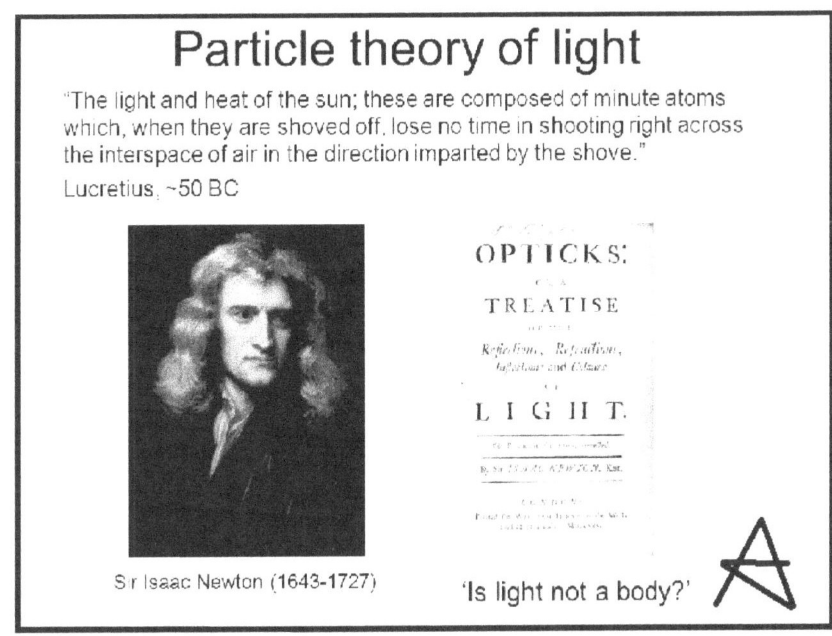

FIG-54: SIR ISSAC NEWTON PROPSED THE PARTICLE THEORY OF LIGHT

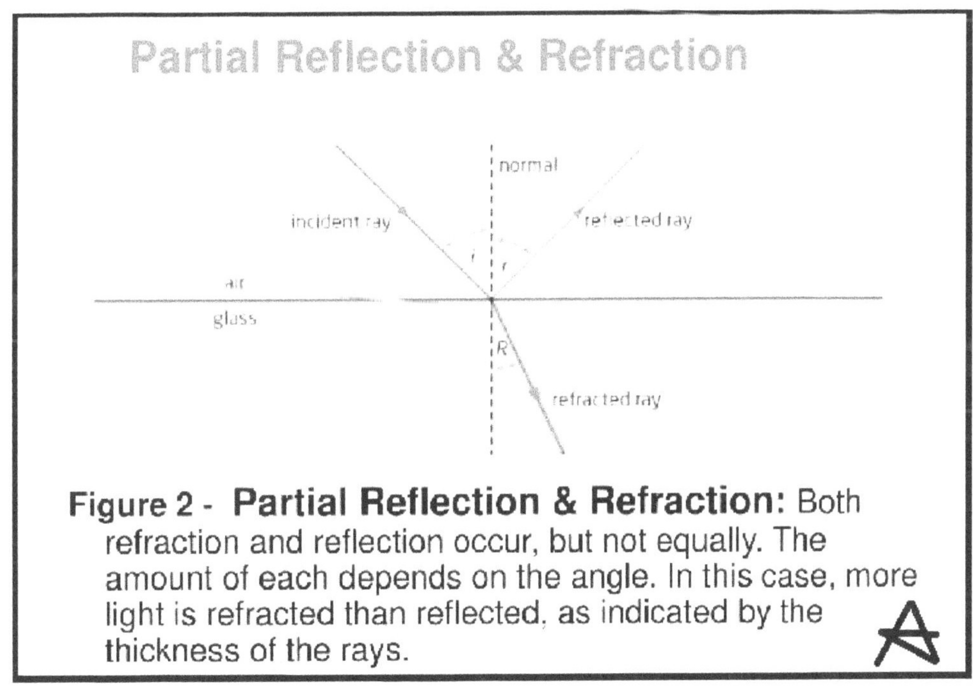

FIG-55: PARTIAL REFLECTION AND REFRACTION OF LIGHT

but later on some of the events like **partial reflection of light,coloured fringes in thin oil-water interfacewere not explained** by assuming corpuscular model of light.so critics challenged this theory but they were suppresses due to authenticity of **sir issac newton.**

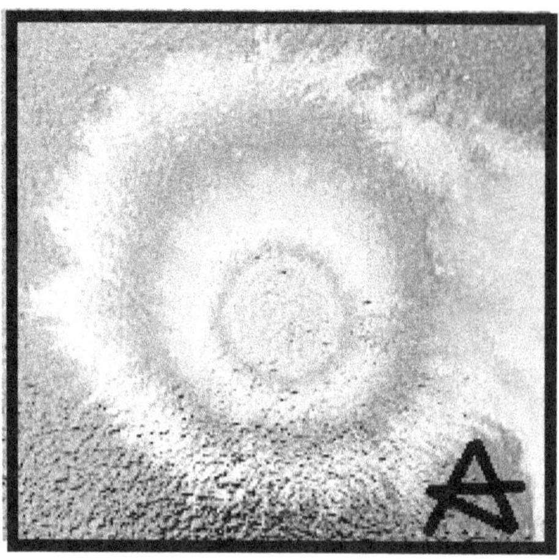

FIG-56: COLOURED FRINGES IN THIN OIL WATER INTERFACE

Sir Christian huygen proposed the **wave theory of light** to explain **partial reflection of light,colours fringes in thin oil-water interface,**but it was initially not accepted becuase of great autheniticity of **sir issac newton**

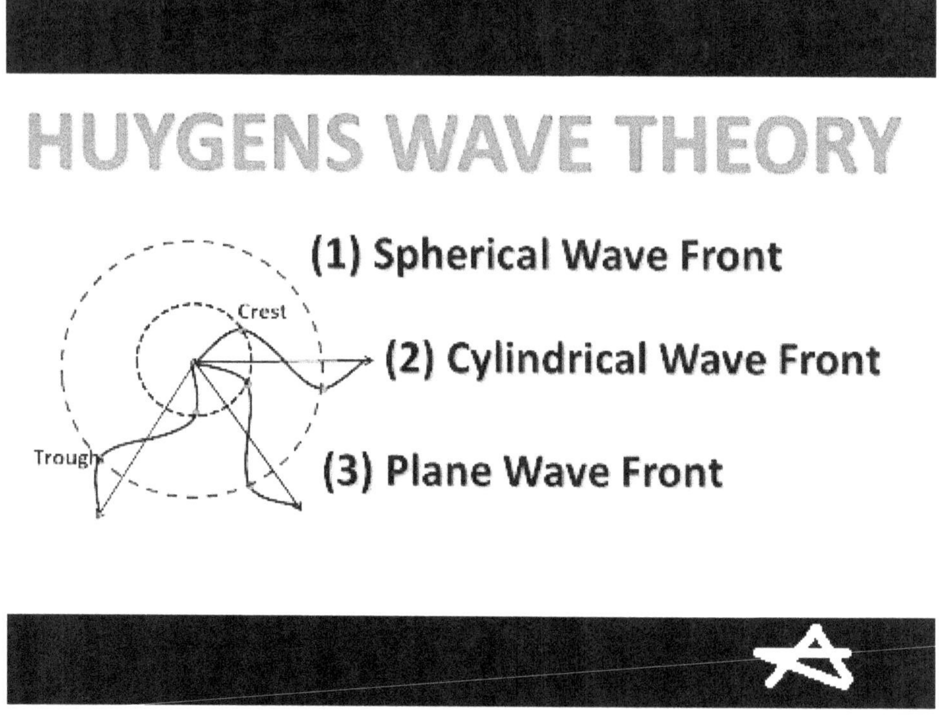

FIG-57: SIR CHRISTIAN HUYGEN PROPOSED THE WAVE THEORY OF LIGHT

However **sir thomas young** performed his famous **double slit experiment in 1801** and proved the **wave theory of light** and all accepted that light has **wave nature**

FIG-58: SIR THOMAS YOUNG'S YDSE EXPERIMENTS

however the wave nature of light was **unable** to explain "PHOTO-ELECTRIC EFFECT" which was explained by **Sir Albert einstein** using "QUANTUM THEORY OF LIGHT" which says that light is made up of particles of energy called as "QUANTAS" or "PHOTON".

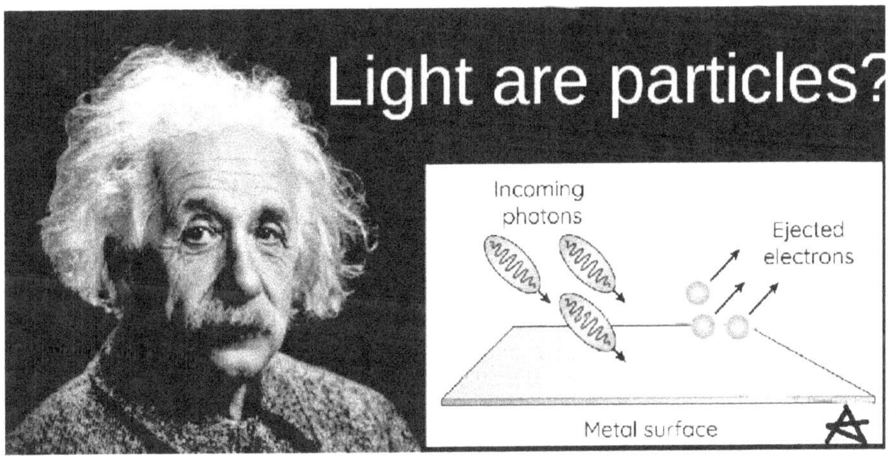

FIG-59: SIR ALBERT EINSTEIN'S PHOTON THEORY OF LIGHT

After that **sir de broglie** proposed the **dual nature of matter and radiations,**and **light is now** assumed to have **both natures** particle as well as wave nature.

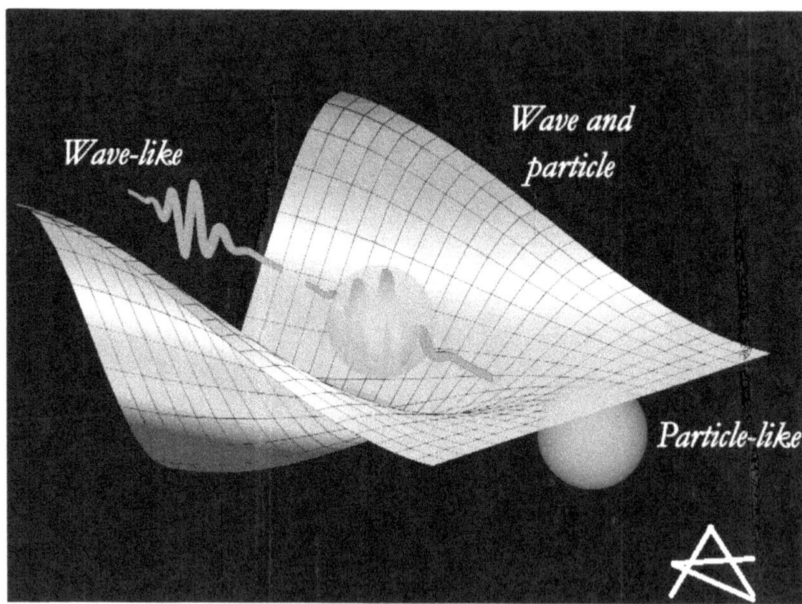

FIG-60: DUAL NATURE OF LIGHT

These series of events lead us to the **conclusion** that **no body is perfect.**Any theory given by anybody is not **perfect.**Any theory is based on **experiments and observations** by somebody.but anybody **don't have access** to all the **dimensions** of an event.

FIG-61: DUAL NATURE OF LIGHT

The universe is always **full of surprises.**things exist beyond what we can contemplate.Most of the space in universe is empty that menas what we know is very small as compared to what we dont know.So we should never be over confident about our knowledge,ratehr we should always work towards betterment of that knowledge for the benifit of our society.

FIG-62: UNIVERSE IS FULL OF SURPRISES

look at this fact in terms of **frequencies.**The universe is fundamentally composed of **strings vibrating withdifferent frequencies.**These **frequencies may vary from zero to infinity,**but everything in the entire universe can be mapped in this domain.

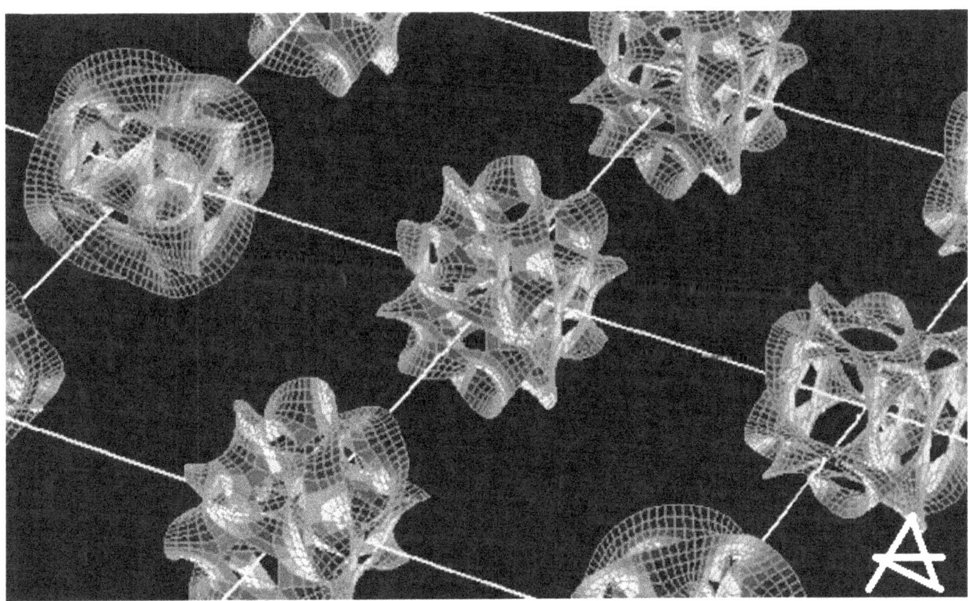

FIG-63: LOOKING AT THE UNIVERSE IN TERMS OF FREQUENCIES

Now a **GENERAL HUMAN BRAIN** has certain limitations.we can listen to sound waves of frequencies varying from **20Hz to 20 Khz,**we can see electromagnetic waves of wavelength from **4000 A to 7500 A.**Hence human brain itself is not capable to operate and detect anything beyond these frequencies.

Things may exist **beyond our limitations.**and **imagination is the doorway** to **unknown frequencies** which is the **fundamental source** of every **known information.**

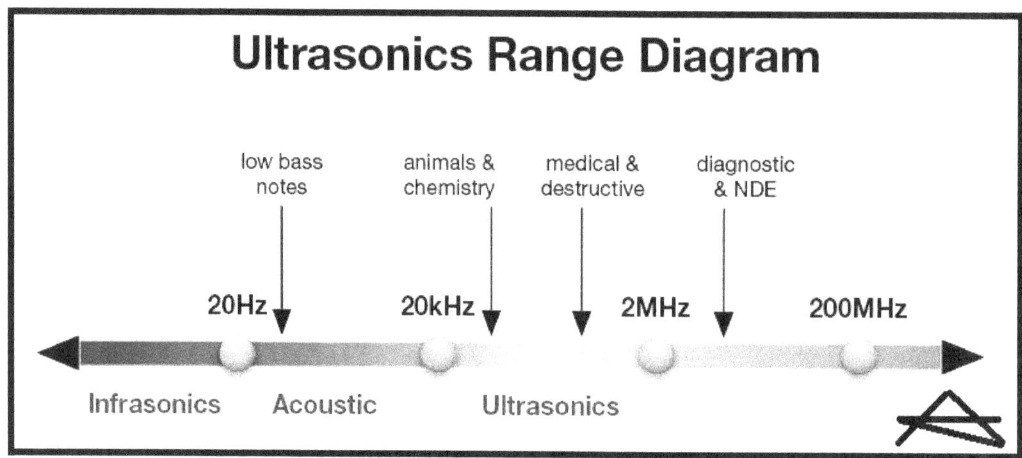

FIG-64: RANGE OF FREQUENCIES OF SOUND WAVES WHICH ARE AUDIBLE

if you want to know things beyond information,**learn meditation** and observe universe.If your **"BRAINWAVES"** can resonate with **gamma waves**, you can know **anything**

FIG-65: LEARN MEDITATION TO KNOW THINGS BEYOND INFORMATION

For more details you can refer to the book
" LIFE BEYOND INFORMATION:KNOW WITHOUT BELEIVING".It's available at amazon.com,flipcart & notionpress.just search for " LIFE BEYOND INFORMATION:KNOW WITHOUT BELEIVING"

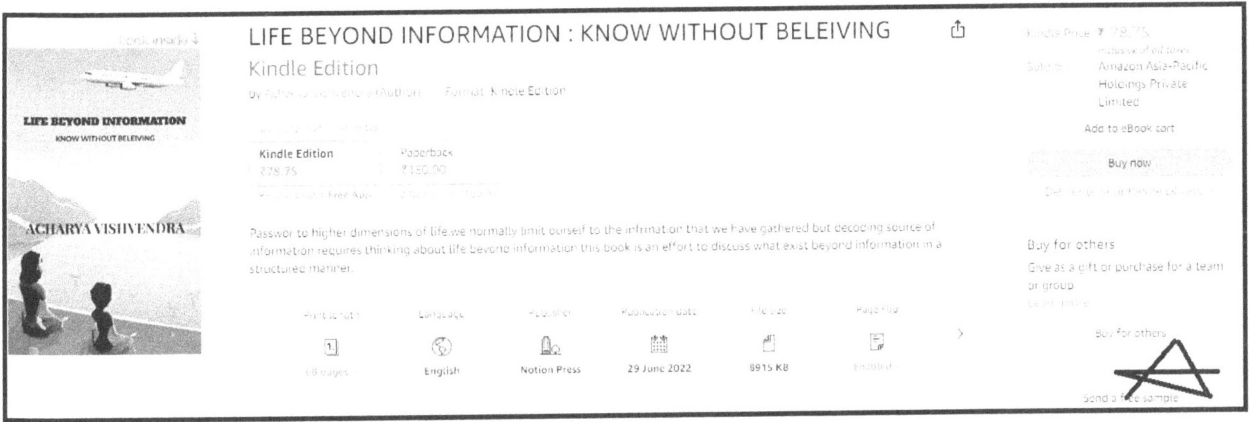

FIG-66: THE BOOK " LIFE BEYOND INFORMATION:KNOW WITHOUT BELEIVING"

Hence we can conclude that imagination skills is an important mental skill necessary for cracking a competitive exam.

Lets discuss **problem solving skills** in the next chapter

CHAPTER SIX

PROBLEM SOLVING SKILL

6.1: After imagination skills,the next skill is the "**PROBLEM SOLVING SKILL**" which is the **core requirement** to crack **competitive exam.**

FIG-67: PROBLEM SOLVING SKILLS

6.2:WHY PROBLEM SOLVING SKILLS ARE NEEDED?

As problems in **competiitve exams** are generally of **new pattern** so you need to have **sharp problem solving skills** to decode the **correct pattern** and implement it in **problems.**

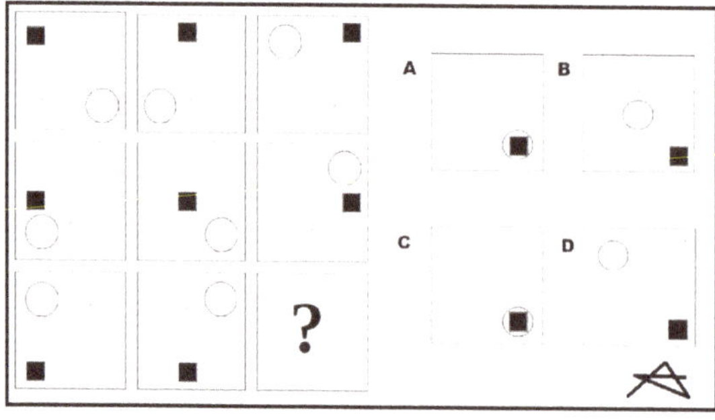

FIG-67: UNKNOWN PATTERNS CAN BE DECODED BY PROBLEM SOLVING

Generally problems asked in **competitive exams** are of **new pattern** which is a combination of the **patterns** that you already know.its just the art of **connecting the new pattern** and its **successful decoding.**

But its a bit **hactic** task.The moment we see a **problem**,the first reaction of the mind is a **flight mode activation.**

Similarly when a student see a new type of problem in **competitive exam**,the first reaction of his **"MIND-BRAIN SYSTEM"** is a **Flight mode activation**.He will feel **fear,anxiety,restlessness,hurry,low energy,depression etc.**and will try to **run away** from **solving the problem.**

This is the reason why **most of the students** fail in **competitive exams** because they are unable to dominate the **flight mode** of the **"MIND-BRAIN SYSTEM"**.and this process **repeats regularly**.every time they see a **different type of question** they gets into the **flight mode** and their **"MIND-BRAIN SYSTEM"** learn to **activate flight mode**,each time they try to solve a **different type of problem.**

Hence students develop the habit of getting into the flight mode and are unable to achieve anything in life as life is always full of problems,such students **boasts a lot** but are unable to even do a **small task** effectively.

FIG-68: FIRST REACTION AFTER SEEING A PROBLEM IS FLIGHT MODE ACTIVATION

FIG-69: FLIGHT MODE & FIGHT MODE ACTIVATION

6.3:STEPS OF PROBLEM SOLVING:

Generally at **psycological level**,problem solving involves **4 steps:**

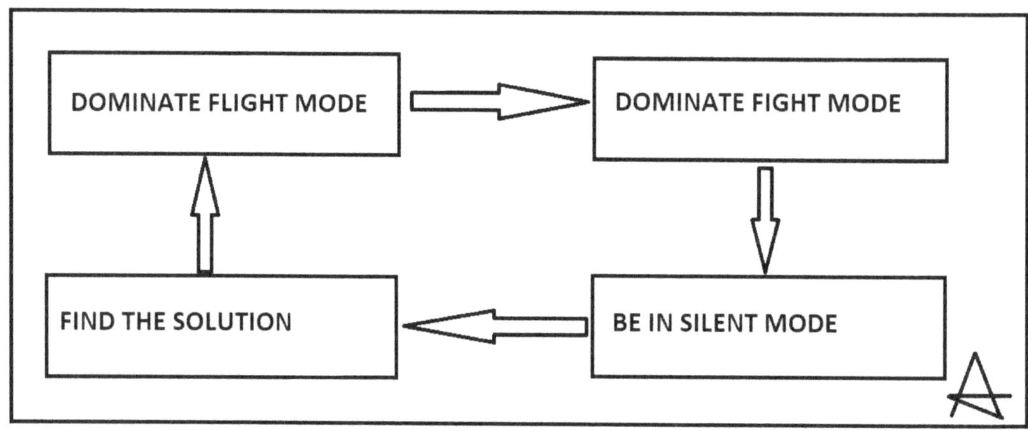

FIG-70: STEPS OF PROBLEM SOLVING

6.3.1.DOMINATE THE FLIGHT MODE:

The first reaction of the "**MIND-BRAIN SYSTEM**" while solving a **question/problem** is activating the **flight mode** and being in a **comfortable state of mind.**you have to dominate the flight mode otherwise you wont be able to find the solution of the problem.Flight mode can be dominated by using a **strong will power** and activating the **manipur chakra.**

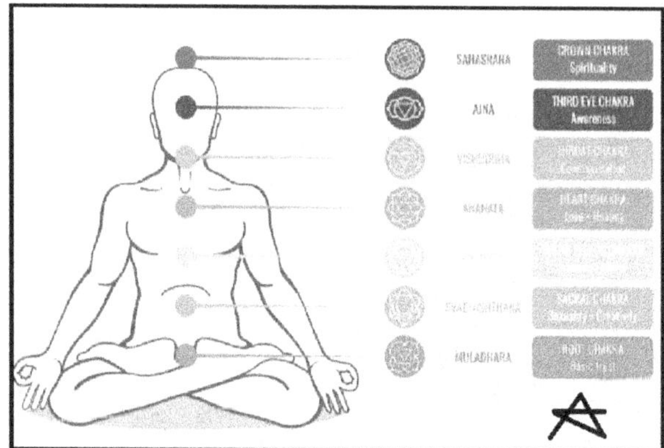

FIG-71:STRONG WILL POWER CAN BE DEVELOPED BY ACTIVATING THE MANIPUR CHAKRA

6.3.2.DOMINATE THE FIGHT MODE:

After dominating the **flight mode,**you have to **fight with the analytical brain,**as **analytical brain** will try to get you back in **comfortable zone.**you will be **safe** but will not get **anything** there.intially you have to fight but you have to **dominate this mode** also as you **can't find solutions** while **fighting.**

FIG-72:IN FLIGHT MODE YOU CAN'T FIND THE SOLUTIONS

6.3.3:ACTIVATE THE SILENT MODE:

After the **flight mode,**the next state is the **state of silent mind** in which you become **thougtless.Silent mind** is very **powerful** and can find solutions **easily.**Make sure you have a **stable silent mind** for **prolonged duration.**only then you will be able to develop yourself as an **effective problem solver** and find **solutions** to your problems asked in **competitive exams.**

FIG-73:ACTIVATE THE SILENT MIND TO FIND THE SOLUTIONS

6.3.4:FIND THE SOLUTION:

After being in **silent mode** you can focus on the **solutions.develop** the solution by following the pattern-**think,plan,implement and write the solution.**

FIG-74:SOLUTIONS CAN BE EASILY FOUND AFTER ACTIVATING THE SILENT MIND

6.4:HOW TO DEVELOP PROBLEM SOLVING SKILLS?

Problem solving skills can't be developed **instantly.**It takes time to **develop these skills.**Start by facing the **problem** and record your **developments.**

For example start with **solving a question** and **note down the observations.**as stated earlier the **first reaction** of your **"MIND-BRAIN SYSTEM"** is a **flight mode activation.**

you will feel **fear,anxiety,restlessness,depression,low feelings** etc but you have to **dominate the flight mode**using **strong will power.**note down the time it takes you to **dominate the flight mode,**

after that your **"MIND-BRAIN SYSTEM"** will activate the **fight mode.**and you will feel **anger,excitement,unstable thoughts,irritation etc.**But you have to **dominate** these feelings using a **strong will power.**

Note down the **time** it takes you to **dominate the fight mode.**if you are able to **dominate the fight mode** you will achieve a **silent state of mind**

and this will activate the **silent mode.**After that you can find **solution**, follow the pattern -**think,plan,implement and write the solution.**

S.N.	DATE	DOMINATE FLIGHT MODE	DOMINATE FIGHT MODE	ACTIVATE SILENT MODE	FIND SOLUTIONS	COMMENTS
1.						
2.						
3.						
4.						
5.						
6.						
7.						
8.						
9.						
10.						
11.						
12.						
13.						
14.						
15.						
16..						
17.						
18.						
19.						
20.						
21.						

FIG-75: DEVELOP PROBLEM SOLVING SKILLS BY FOLLOWING 21 DAYS PRACTICE

Initially you will have to struggle with your **analytical brain** but dominate all resistances with a **strong will power** and gradually you will develop **sharp problem solving skills.**

FIG-76: HAVE A STRONG WILL POWER TO DOMINATE ANALYTICAL BRAIN

CHAPTER SEVEN

BRAINWAVE FREQUENCY MODULATION SKILL

7.1:After learning **problem solving skills** the next skills that you need to learn is **brainwave frequency modulation skill.**

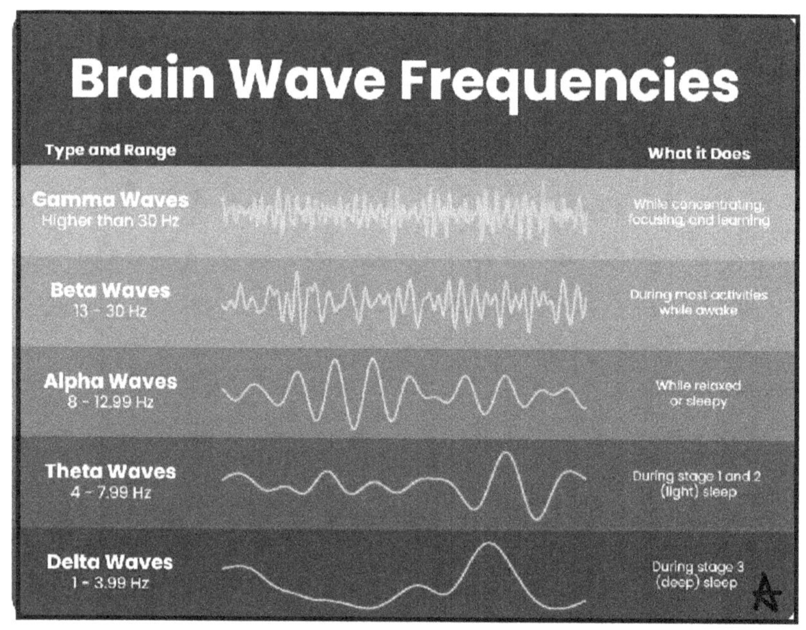

FIG-77: DIFFERENT BRAIN WAVE FREQUENCIES

7.2:WHY YOU NEED TO LEARN BRAINWAVE FREQUENCY MODULATION SKILLS?

as stated earlier for being **successful** in competitive exams like **JEE,NEET,UPSC,CUET,ICAR,NTSE,KVPY** you need to solve problems asked in the **competitive** exam **JEE,NEET,UPSC,CUET,ICAR,NTSE,KVPY.**

Solving a problem asked in **competitive exams** is very different from solving a problem in school exam.As in school exams very **limited information** is to be learn and a very **few patterns** are there.so its easy to score **good in school exams** whereas the problems asked in **competitive exams** are **multi-dimensional** and includes a **huge information base** and a large number of **patterns.**For solving these problems you need to develop your "**MIND-BRAIN SYSTEM**" for processing **multi-dimensional problems** which involves using **different parts of the brain** in a **proper sequence** to arrive at the **solution.**

For example:To solve a typical question asked in Jee physics you need to use memory,analysis,imagination and calculations.refer to the below figure for details.

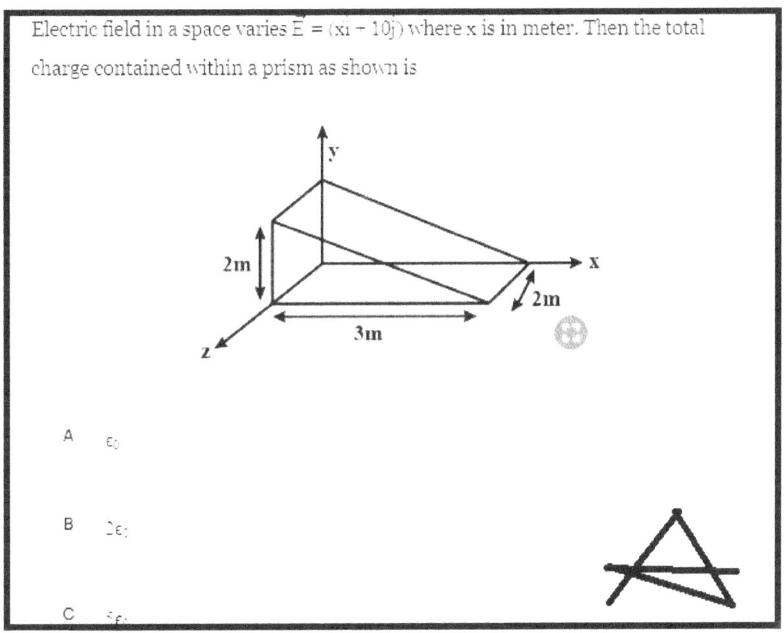

FIG-78: A TYPICAL PROBLEM FOR JEE PHYSICS

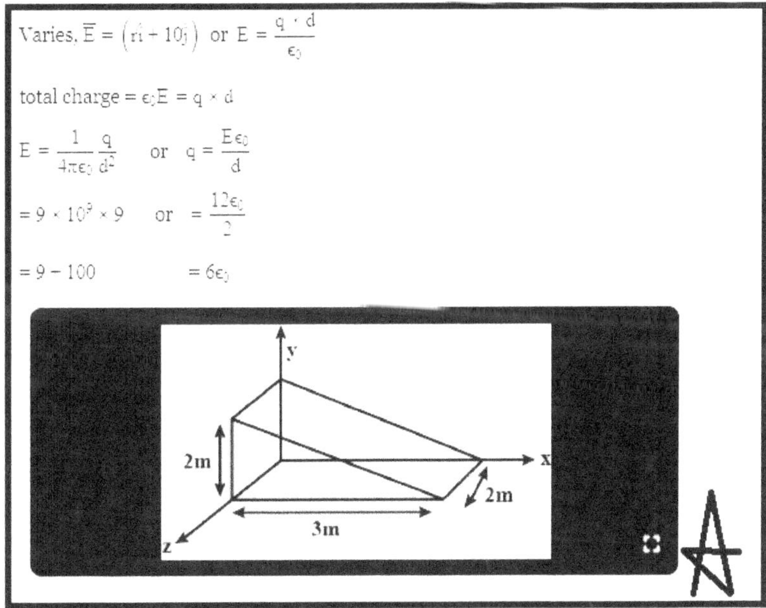

FIG-79: SOLUTION FOR A TYPICAL JEE PHYSICS PROBLEM

Now **memory** is concerned with the **temporal lobe** where as **analysis is concerned with the frontal lobe** so to solve a problem for **competitive exam** you need to use **different lobes** and these different lobes operate at **different frequencies.**so you need to learn the art of **brainwave frequency modulation** so that you can use different lobes of the brain as and when needed according to the question/problem

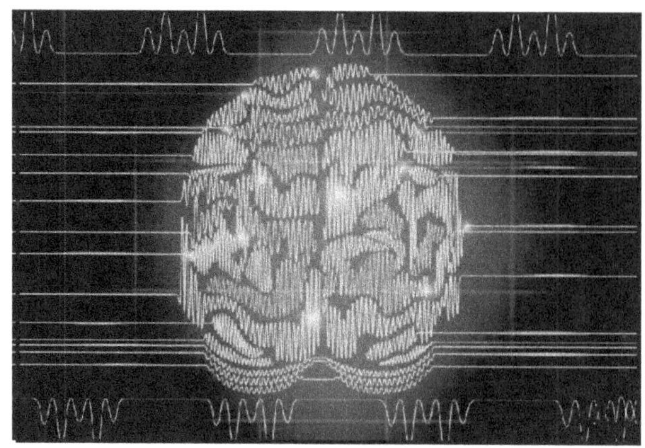

FIG-80: DIFFERENT PARTS OF THE BRAIN ARE ACTIVATED AT DIFFERENT FREQUENCIES

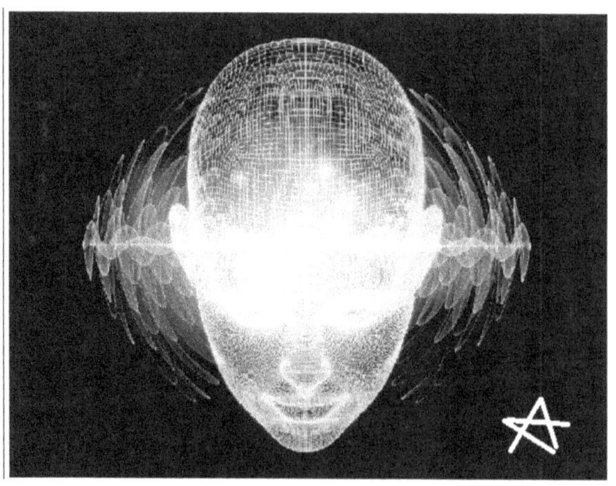

FIG-81: DIFFERENT PARTS OF THE BRAIN ARE ACTIVATED AT DIFFERENT FREQUENCIES

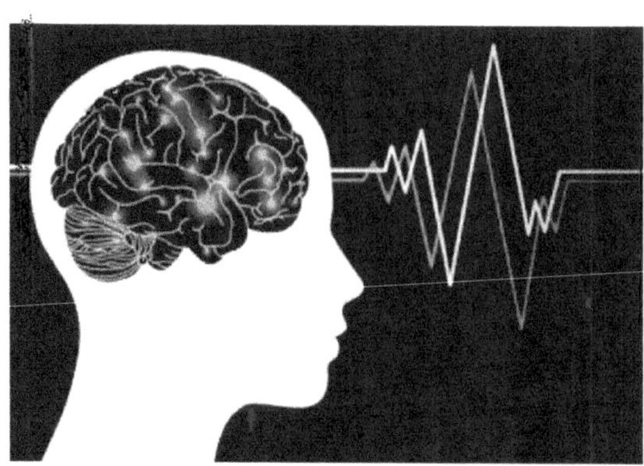

FIG-82: DIFFERENT MENTAL PROCESSES TAKES PLACE AT DIFFERENT BRAINWAVE FREQUENCIES

FIG-83: OUR THOUGHT PATTERN CHANGES WITH CHANGE IN BRAINWAVE FREQUENCY

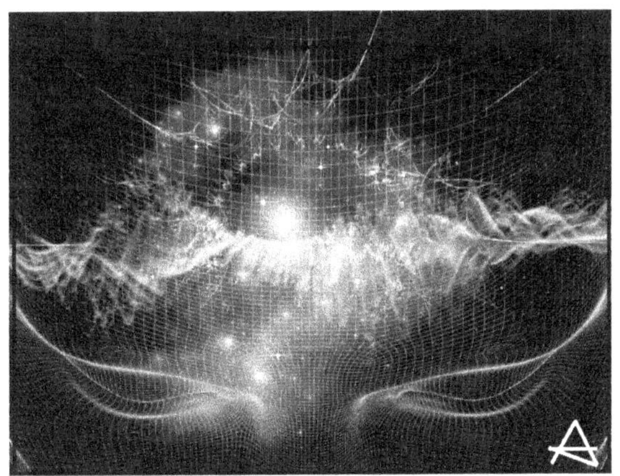

FIG-84: OUR SELF PERCEPTION CHANGES WITH CHAGE IN BRAINWAVE FREQUENCY

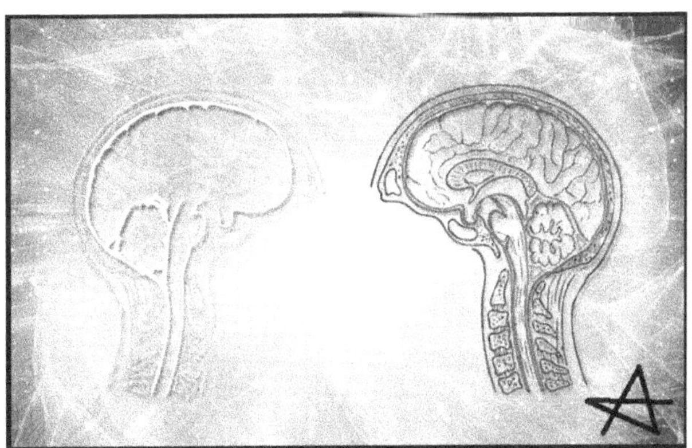

FIG-85:INTERCONNECTION OF 3 MINDS TAKES PLACE AT HIGHER BRAINWAVE FREQUENCIES

7.3:HOW TO LEARN BRAINWAVE FREQUENCY MODULATION SKILLS?

Brain wave frequency modulation is an art.it can be learnt with gradual practice for at least **21 days.**generally while doing normal work our brainwave frequency resonates with **Beta waves** but to solve problems of **competitive exams** we need to increase the brainave frequency to **gamma waves.**

S.N.	DATE	Beta wave activation	comments
1.			
2.			
3.			
4.			
5.			
6.			
7.			
8.			
9.			
10.			
11.			
12.			
13.			
14.			
15.			
16..			
17.			
18.			
19.			
20.			
21.			

FIG-86: LEARN BRAINWAVE FREQUENCY MODULATION IN 21 DAYS

so gradually practice to operate at **higher brainwave frequency.**your **analytical brain** will oppose you in increasing the **brain-wave frequency.**so you have to dominate your **analytical brain** by using **will power** and soon you will learn the **art of brainwave frequency modulaion** and will be able to use different parts of the brain as and when needed to solve a problem asked in competitive exam.

FIG-87: DOMINATE ANALYTICAL BRAIN BY WILL POWER

Let's discuss **Strong will power skill** in the next chapter in details.

STRONG WILL POWER SKILL

8.1:"STRONG WILL" is the foundation of success in cracking **competitive exam.**As preparng for a **competitive exam** is a long process so there are **ups and downs,mood swings,distractions,deviations etc** and all of these can be dominated only by a **strong will power.**

FIG-88: STRONG WILL POWER

8.2:WHY STRONG WILL POWER IS NEEDED?

As explained earlier there are **distractions** in the path way,**many issues** can arise when you will start preparing for **competitive exams** which can be dominated only by having a **strong will power.**

if your will power is low,distractions will deviate you,in fact inside you there exist negative energy which will try to pull you down from achieving your targets.you have to fight with that negative energy and for that you need to have avery strong will power.

FIG-89:WHY STRONG WILL POWER IS NEEDED?

8.2:HOW TO DEVELOP A STRONG WILL POWER?

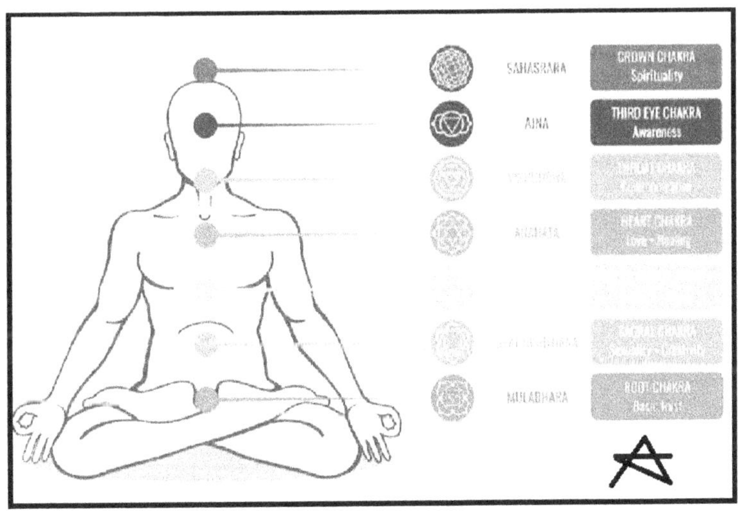

FIG-90:HOW TO DEVELOP STRONG WILL POWER?

Will power is concerned with the **manipur/solar plexux chakra.**if you feel that you have a **weak will power** then you need to **activate your manipur chakra.**This can be done with **meditation.**

To learn meditation,you can refer to **the book "DEVELOPING MIND,DEVELOP INDIA".**This book is available online at **amazon,flipcart & notionpress.**

FIG-91:THE BOOK "DEVELOPING MIND,DEVELOP INDIA"

Lets discuss the last skill which requires the combined effect of all the **previous skills** and **called as** the **optimal performance skill.**

CHAPTER NINE

OPTIMAL PERFORMANCE SKILL

9.1:You are known by your **performance** in life.If you can **perform** you can achieve **anything.**So **optimal performance/peak performance** is the **last skill** that we need to learn in order to crack a **competiitve exam.**

9.2:WHY OPTIMAL PERFORMANCE SKILL IS NEEDED?

You must have realised that solving a question at home sitting comfortably is easy whereas if the same question is solved in **front of class** or during **exam** then it seems to be a **bit difficult.**Its because when we perform before others we are concenred about the **output/result/image.**We may be internally less **intelligent** but we preptend to be **more intelligent** than we are,this **disturbs the brain** and **interfere in its functioning,** which decrease **our concentration power in performance.**

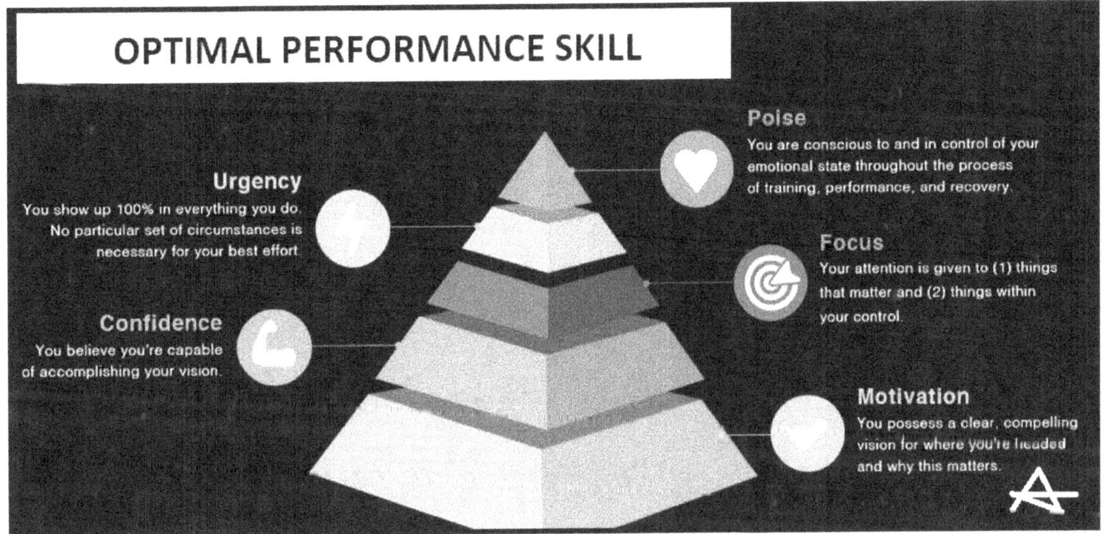

FIG-92: OPTIMAL PERFORMANCE SKILL

This **distraction** can be overcome only by **adaptation to different testing environment** by giving a lot of **mock tests** and using a **strong will power** to **increase our concentration power.**

FIG-93: APPEARING FOR MOCK TESTS DEVELOPS OPTIMAL PERFORMANCE SKILLS

So **optimal performance skills** are needed to learn how to bear the brunt of **exam pressure** and perform to your **best.**

FIG-94: OPTIMAL PERFORMANCE SKILLS CAN BE DEVELOPED WITH GRADUAL PRACTICE

9.3:HOW TO DEVELOP OPTIMAL PERFORMANCE SKILLS?

It has been observed **experimentally** that **optimal performance** occurs at **optimal stress level** which is **different for different students** with **too less stress** or **too much stress,**performace is not **optimal** as shown by the below figureso students must decode their **optimal stress** and try to work at that **stress level.**

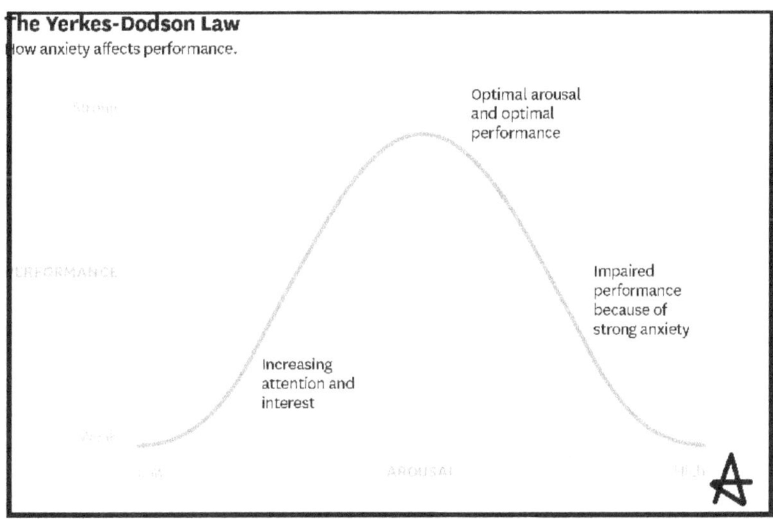

FIG-95: OPTIMAL PERFORMANCE TAKES PLACE AT OPTIMAL STRESS

Developing optimal performance skills is not an instantaneous effect.it takes time to develop it.start with a **21 days Mock test schedule.**Note down your **performance and stress level** and try to **decode your optimalstress.**

S.N.	DATE	OPTIMAL STRESS	comments
1.			
2.			
3.			
4.			
5.			
6.			
7.			
8.			
9.			
10.			
11.			
12.			
13.			
14.			
15.			
16..			
17.			
18.			
19.			
20.			
21.			

FIG-96: TAKE 21 MOCK TESTS AND TRY TO DECODE YOUR OPTIMAL STRESS

Hence these were some mental skills which you must have for cracking competitive exams.Most of the students fail in competiitve exams because they don't have mental skills compatible to crack the competitive exam.So its our belief that this book will prove to be a boon to the students who aspire to crack the competitive exam but don't have sharp skills.by developing these mental skills you can be successful in competitive exams and further in your professional and spiritual life.

All the best for your competitive exams

Acharya vishvendra

Our Other Information Sources

1.BOOKS:

We have compiled more than **100 books** for **jee & neet,educational psycology,metaphysics & spiritualism.**

Search **"ACHARYA VISHVENDRA"** on **Amazon,flipcart & notionpress** to get access to our books.

These books are avilable in kindle format/soft copy as well as printed format/hard copy

For soft copy visit **Amazon app** or **amazon.in** website

For hard copy visit **Notionpress.com**

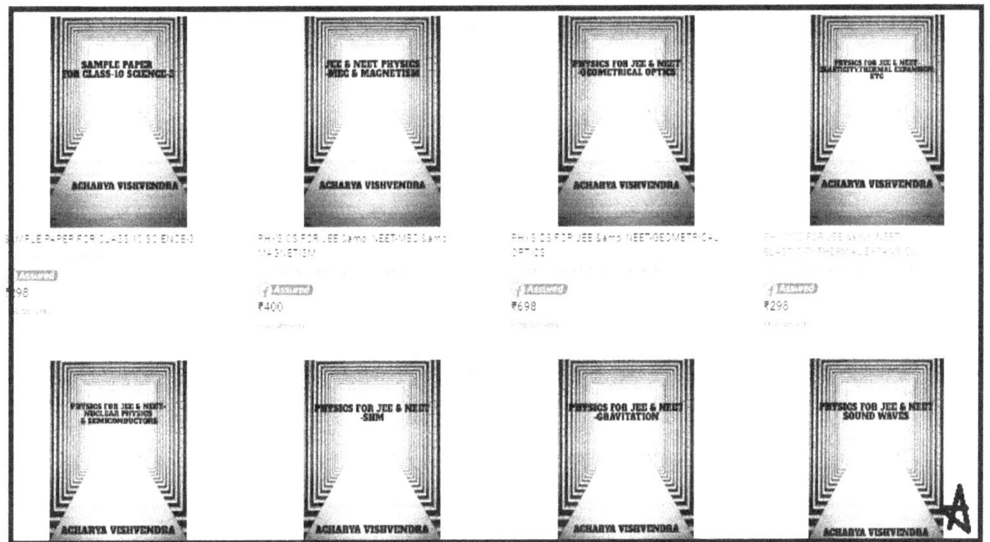

FIG-97: OUR BOOKS ON FLIPCART

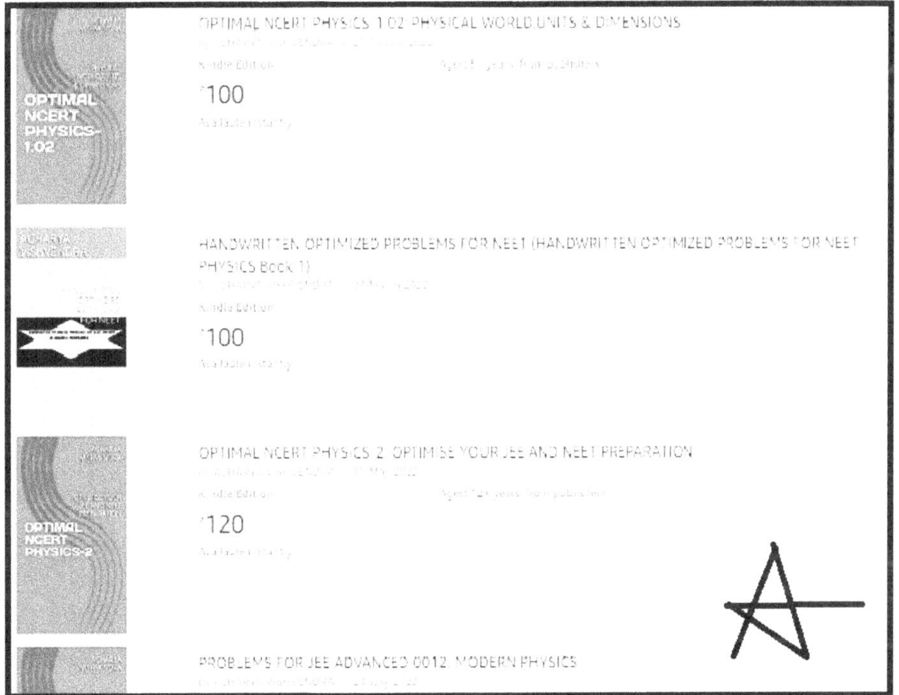

FIG-98: OUR BOOKS ON AMAZON

FIG-99: OUR BOOKS ON NOTIONPRESS

2.YOU-TUBE VIDEO LECTURES:

We have our official you-tube channel as below:

ACHARYA VISHVENDRA You can search these on **you-tube** and get access to **hundreds of videos** on different topics for **Jee & neet & educational psycology.**

FIG-100: OUR OFFICIAL YOU-TUBE CHANNEL"ACHARYA VISHVENDRA"

We have tried our best to keep this book error free,however human efforts are never perfect,there are always chances of improvement.if readers find any error or have any feedback then kindly drop us an e-mail at:**acharyavishvendra@gmail.com**